DO NOT READ!
PRIVATE INFORMASHON!

This is my life story. Every single diarrhe i ever wrote taped together to make a relly good Book for myself to reed.

FOR MY EYEBALLS ONLY!!!
Do NOT REED UNLESS YOU ARE ME!

This Book is full of Private informashon that could RUIN my Life if any1 ever read it. My BaBy Book, my Prayer journal, my emotional teenage meltdowns, My Boyfriend drama, and even my Favorite snacks. ALL my secrets.

So do NOT reed this Book unless you are ME!
Thank you.
Bye.

My Diarrhe

Miranda Sings

SIMON & SCHUSTER

London · New York · Sydney · Toronto · New Delhi

A CBS COMPANY

First published in the United States by Gallery Books, an imprint of Simon & Schuster, Inc., 2018
First published in Great Britain by Simon & Schuster UK Ltd, 2018
A CBS COMPANY

1 3 5 7 9 10 8 6 4 2

Simon & Schuster UK Ltd
1st Floor
222 Gray's Inn Road
London WC1X 8HB

www.simonandschuster.co.uk
www.simonandschuster.com.au
www.simonandschuster.co.in

Simon & Schuster Australia, Sydney
Simon & Schuster India, New Delhi

The author and publishers have made all reasonable efforts to contact copyright-holders for permission, and apologise for any omissions or errors in the form of credits given. Corrections may be made to future printings.

A CIP catalogue record for this book is available from the British Library

Hardback ISBN: 978-1-4711-7206-9
eBook ISBN: 978-1-4711-7208-3

Printed in Italy

Miranda Sings
Jan 1, 2018
4:29 pm

Dear Diarrhe,

GUESS WHAT?!? I Found all my old diarrhe's from my Whole Entire Life when i was Looking for a snack underneeth my Bed. So i decided to tape them all together to make one huge **BOOK** that i can read whenever i want 2 remember all the memories i remember from my Memory that i can remember. So this is Basicaly my **AUTOBIOGRAFY**.

Too Bad their is so many secrets in it or else i culd sell it and make a ~~FORCHUN~~ FORTUNE!

ANYWAYS, my foot is ichy so i shuld probly go. Bye.

Miranda

P.S. i Found 4 cheeseBalls under my Bed. SCORE!

Jan 1, 2018
4:41 pm

i would lick 2 dedicate this Book to **Myself** cuz im the only person who is allowed 2 read it.

im serius. if you are reading this and you are NOT me, STOP iT **RITE** **NOW!** i will make you regret it SO HARD. Thank you.

Miranda
Jan 1, 2018
4:52 pm

Tabel of Contents

Jan 1, 2018
6:31 PM

ABOUT THE AUTHER

Miranda Sings is

a incredibel singer, dancer, actor, model, magichan, etc. She alredy has a #1 [redacted] New York Times Best selling Book, 2 seasons of her own Netflix original series, and many sold out world tours. She also has a cat. She is the most amazing, incredibel, pefect, Beautiful, smart, talented genius in the world. she is also humble.

—miranda sings

Quotes from celeBrities—

"this is the best book I ever read."

- Miranda Sings

Miranda Sings
Jan 1, 2018
6:58 PM
DO NOT
READ!
PRIVATE
infourma
shon

Miranda Sings
Jan 1, 2018
7:00 PM

UNLESS ur name is

Miranda Sings

and you look like this

PUT. THE BOOK **DOWN**!!!!!!!!

miranda Sings
Jan 2, 2018
11:01 am

IM NOT KiDDING!
STOP READING
RITE NOW!!!

Miranda Sings
Jan 2, 2018
11:04 AM

Ok, now that its just me - Hi Miranda. you look very grate today. enjoy your Book on you.

♡, you.

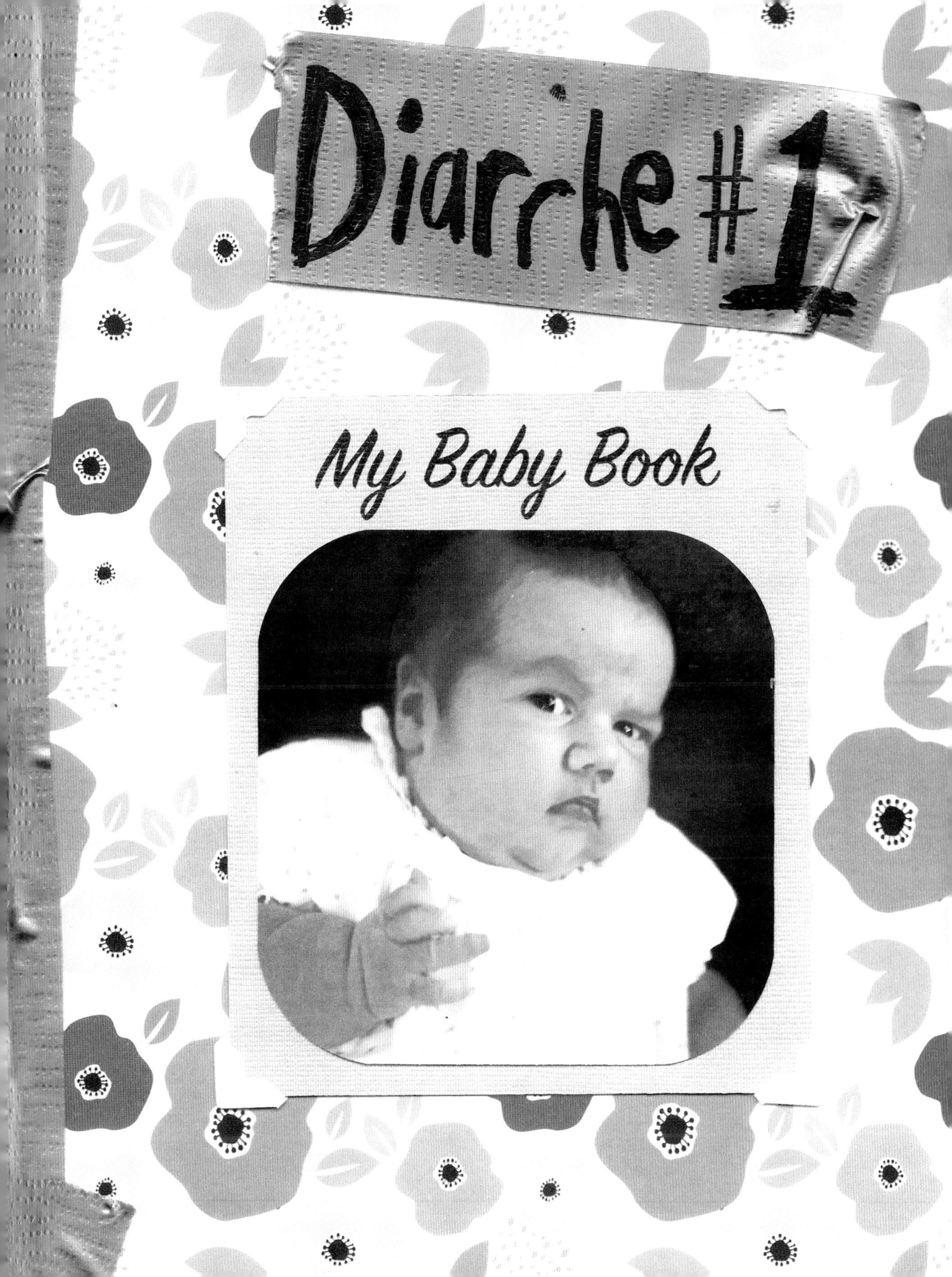
Diarrhe #1
My Baby Book

← 2018 Miranda Talking

Miranda Sings
Jan 2, 2018
12:09 PM

OK, so i no this is tecknickly my **BaBy Book** and not a **Diarrhe**, Butt i was reading it and notised my mom got ALOT of stuf **WRONG!** So i had to fix it and now its a very educatchonal Book about me as a Baby. or as i Like to call it → **My AfterBirth**.

FYI - every time you see **RED PEN** marks, its me NOW Fixing my moms dumb mistakes so NOW, please enjoy,

My AfterBirth.

My First Photograph

This mite Be Barf, Butt i think its my Breth From singing so HARD

Fixed my Listick

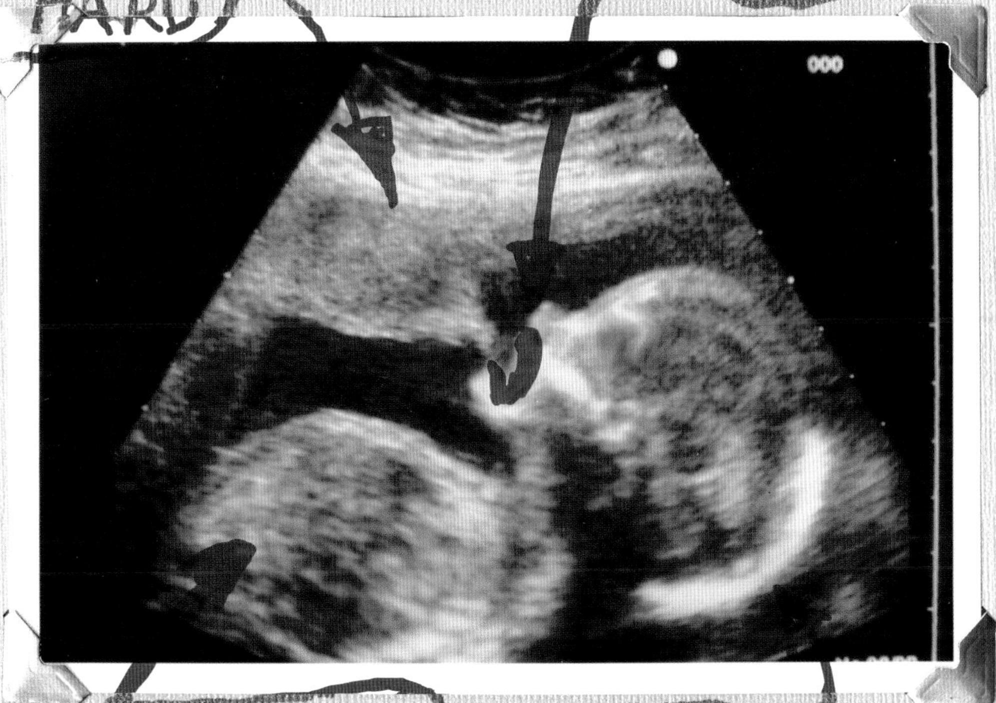

The Photografer For this photo shoot was NOT GOOD! This pic is so BLURRY!

BABY

i Lived in my moms tookie Before i was Born so i dont even wanna know how he got inside to take this pitchur.

It's a Girl

My Arrival

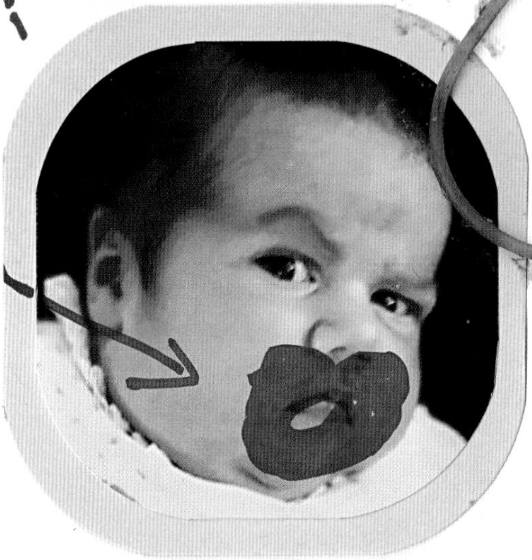

i wasnt waring any Lipstick so i fixed it.

oops. i spilled some Brekfast.

wow! I was 114 pounds wen i was borned and now im 124. i only gained 10 pounds sinse Birth! skinny legend.

Date of birth Dec 24, 19

Time of birth 9:34 AM ← This is A LIE! i never Been awake that early BeFORE.

Weight 11.4 pounds!

Length 22 inches ← im at least 24 inches now.

Eye color Black ← rasist.

Hair color Brown ← no. it was DARK BROWN!!

Distinguishing characteristics

~~LOUD! Lots of hair.~~

relly pretty. Gunna Be FAMUS!

My First Footprint
Fixed it.

My First Bath

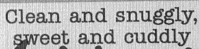

Clean and snuggly,
sweet and cuddly

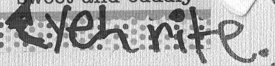

yeh rite

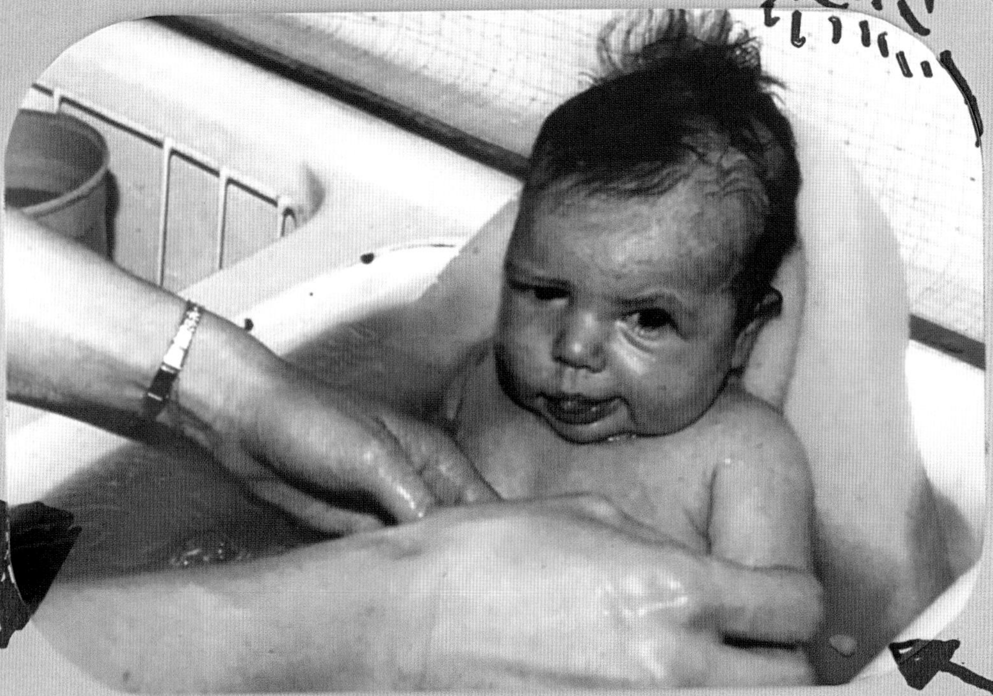

see? corn!

i LOVE sink Baths! Mom always washed me after doing dishes so sometimes there was Bonus scraps of food floating in the water!

My First Word

Miranda said her first word today. She pointed at me and said, "dumb." Now that is what she calls me. She's been doing it all day.

Model.

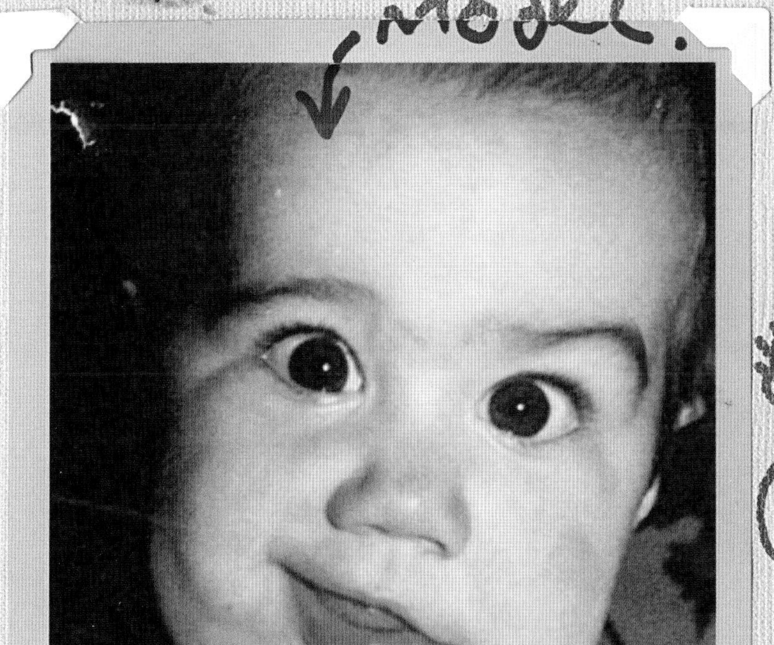

sweet Baby

obviusly I always been relly smart.

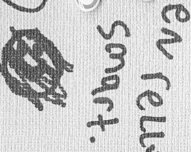

My First Haircut

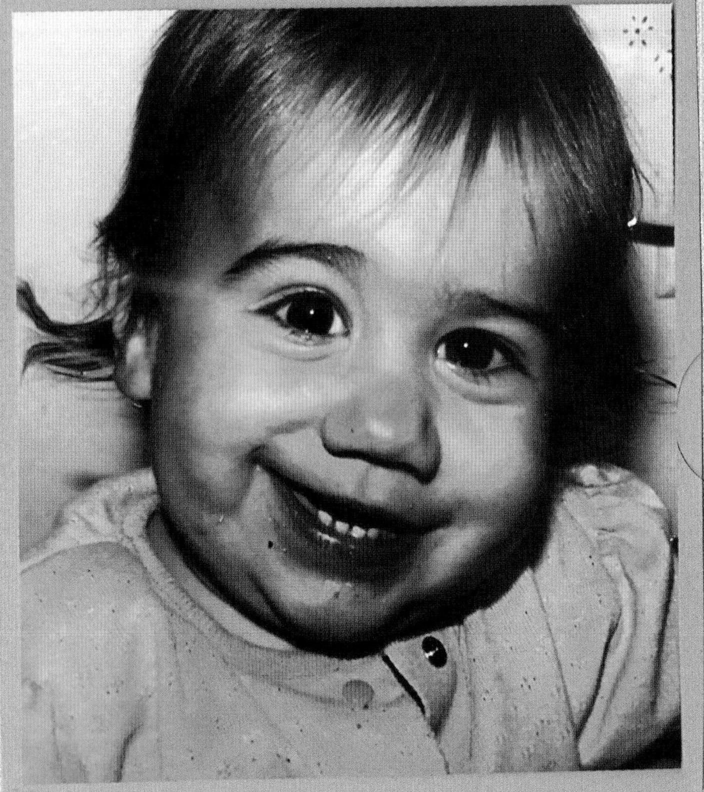

This hare is Kinda yellow Butt mine is Brown so i colord it in to mach my real hare

my actual → hare From 2day. i wanted 2 compare it with the baby hair. its a match!

My First Bed

Miranda refuses to sleep in her crib so she just sleeps on the floor whenever she pleases. I think she likes the Master Bedroom best so I'm currently moving out of it so she can have it. Having a baby is such an adventure! So fun. so neat. so... so... fun...

i cant Believe my mom Let people walk on my Bed! Literally SO RUDE!

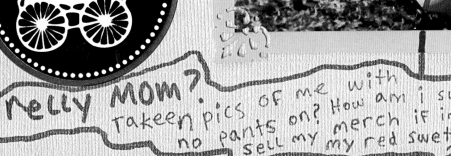

relly MOM?. takeen pics of me with no pants on? How am i supposed 2 sell my merch if im not waring my red swetpants 24/7?

I don't like...

My Mom 4got a lot of stuff on this list. i Fixed it

sleeping	smiling
Being held	Being touched
hugs	Playgrounds
being looked at	My mommy's hugs
being talked to	Haters, Birds, Fruit,
diapers	vegtibles, old people, porn style clothes,
Babies	Living cats, aliens, Chia pets that dont
Animals	grow fast, when i dont have eye crunchies in
People	the morning, Owen, Bangs, lettuce,
Baths	DULL KNives, when people dont RT me,
Being dirty	mustard, toothpaste, drugs, chestical cracks,
Being clean	iChy panties, spicy things, when you poo
Toys	and have to wipe a million times, Colleen,
laughing	This Baby Book, people who talk to me when i

have my headphones in, all other people, Trump, the smell of chocolat, working, exersize, Lerning, hate comments, santa Claus, and etc.

I like...

Eating.

Big News!

Miranda's going to be a BIG SISTER

NO!

This never happened!!!!!

My Favorite Snack

She didnt menchon my Fav snaks NOW. i LiCK meat and chees BaLLS

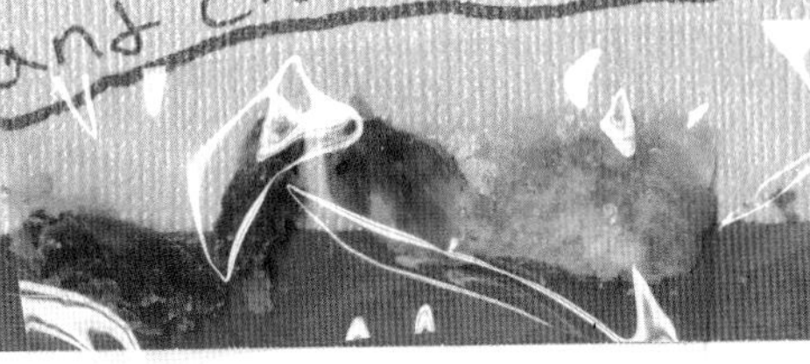

Ive tried everything to get her to stop eating snails, but she loves them. Ive heard rich people like them so I think it means she has very expensive taste. Isn't that neat?

ooh! i remember this one. it had Lots OF BUBBLES wich made it extra squitshy and delitchus

My First Friend

Miranda finally made a friend! I paid the neighbor to let me babysit her daughter for an hour. She cried the entire time and Miranda loved it! I love seeing my baby girl smile.

I cant Beleve my mom did this. calling me a BABY wen im obviusLy like 4 or [redacted] 5?? child abuse!

OK, lets get 1 thing straight. This girl was NOT my Frend. I would NEVER be Frends w/ ANY1 who has BANGS Like that. Shes obviusLy a murderer.

My First Poo

splish splash

Thats a good one.

all wet!

cute

sweet

My First Pet

bundle

all Girl

i Fixed my Listick
and hare.

This cat was SO RUDE! He ran away the day after i stole him from our nayBor's house.

relly, mom? Takeen pics of me with no pants ~~AGAIN?~~ i drew some on. Gotta sell that merch! www.mirandaSings.com

This snake was dum. He wuldnt stay on my neck Like a necklase so i set him Free By FLUShing him down the toiLet.

i Finaly got a pet that i LOVED. He was my BFF. Charlie the FLy. i dont no whos Bunny that is. i hate animols. gross.

My First ~~Sister~~

i dont have a sister

Miranda trying to break her ~~sister's~~ swing. Such a silly girl! :)

This is the first time the girls touched. [redacted] started crying and then Miranda threw up. They haven't touched since...

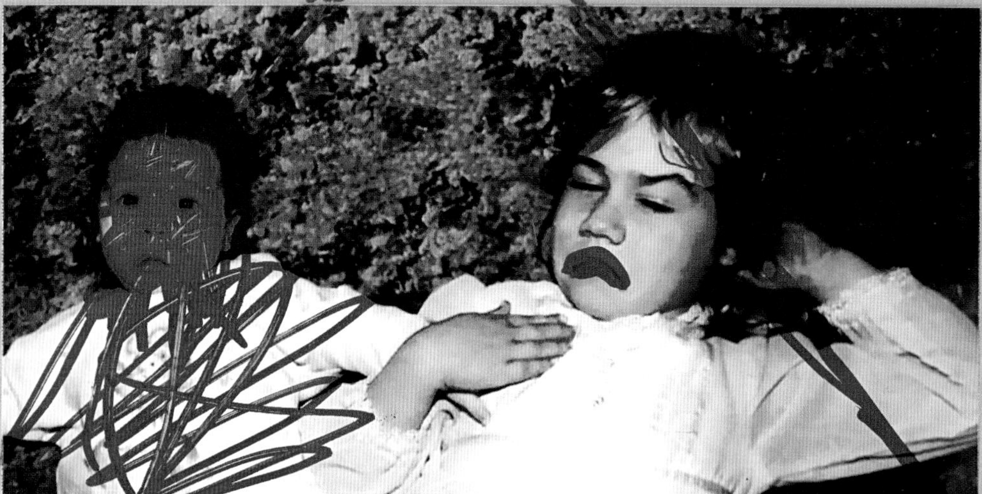

Holiday Memories

The only holiday that matters is my Birthday and its Not on Here!!

Miranda did a four hour concert before letting the family open their gifts. She's so thoughtful.

4th Of July

Miranda wasn't happy about ~~her sister~~ getting a Christmas Present.

A fun Easter performance! Miranda is about to crucify herself. So cute.

Performing Memories

im Hungry.

Miranda has put on hundreds of plays and won countless TONY AWARDS (made by me of course.) Here are some of my favorite Performances...

WHAT. Those weren't REAL?!

Me and GOD wrote this play. i Lived in that tomb 4 3 days. it was cold

BIBLE the Musical

Jesus Christ Superstar

Sound of Music

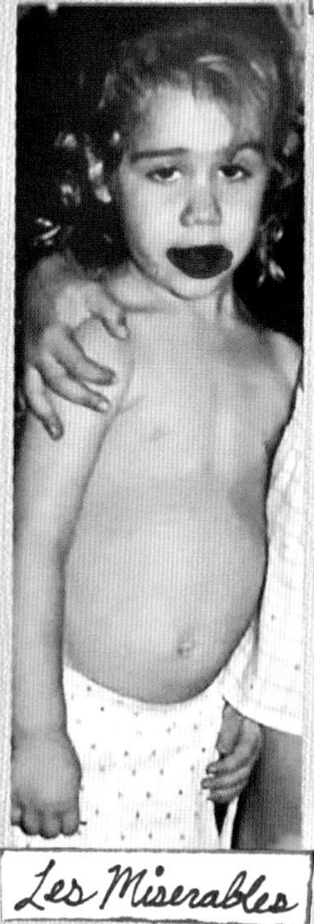

Les Miserables

Sweenie Todd

every single Performance was sold out my mom was a gr8 audient.

Happy Memories

Miranda is happiest when she's eating ← TRUE.

a big chunk of meat.... delitchus.

Ew. who force fed me a vegtibl

Silly Memories

I asked Miranda to pick up her toys and she ran outside and did this. She's so silly.

This is NOT silly. its SERIUS! if you Boss me around their will be consiquenses.

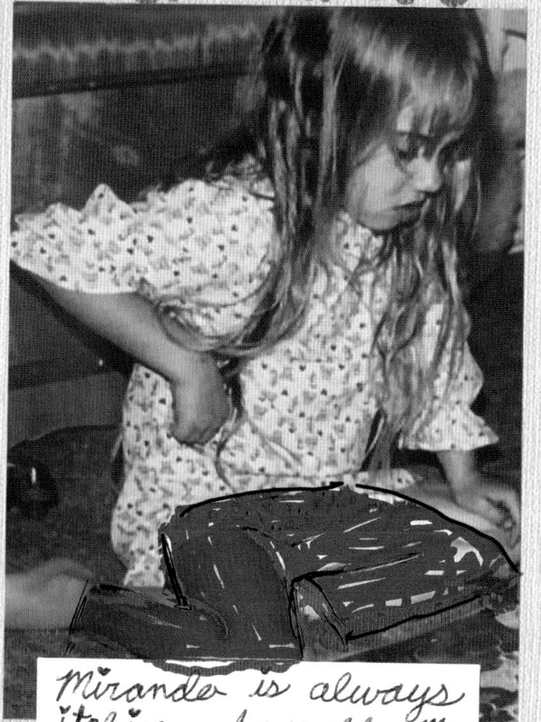

Miranda is always itching herself. My itchy little angel. Silly Girl!

This is Miranda's favorite T.V. program. I don't know what it is but it seems fun.. and silly!

This is TeriFying! I Cant Beleve i was wearing Pigtails! So Scary.

Miranda hugged me for the first time ever today. It made me cry. I will cherish that moment for the rest of my life.
I love you, Miranda.

Love You too Mom.

Diarrhe #2
Miranda's Schoolwork

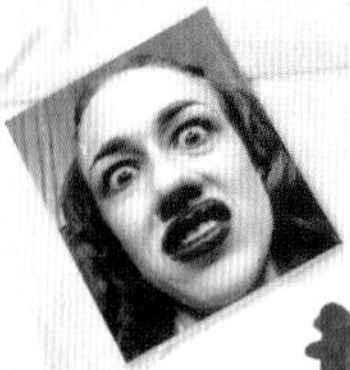

Miranda Sings
Jan 2, 2018
3:21 pm

Diarrhe #2 is my homeschool workBOOK. in this journal, i discover my talents, meet my Best Frend, and Learn Stuff.

Dear Bethany,

I regret to inform you that we can no longer have Miranda in our first grade classroom. She has continued to be quite problematic and I'm afraid we are not qualified to deal with a child with this many behavioral issues. We assumed you would discipline your daughter after we informed you that she "accidentally" flushed the class hamster down the toilet, and then urinated on the magic reading carpet for a week because she "didn't want the hamster to steal her pee."

It is obvious to us that you haven't dealt with this issue as we have noticed her behavior has gotten worse. She will not allow anyone to speak unless they are complimenting her, she is constantly singing and dancing on desks while I am trying to teach, and she locks children in the toy chest if they don't applaud for her all day long. Today she forced all of the students to lay on their stomachs on the playground to create a "stage" that she could tap dance on. Two students have broken fingers, one has a black eye, and Mrs. Srickland is still locked in the broom closet after Miranda superglued it shut so she wouldn't stop her performance. While we appreciate Miranda's confidence and bold personality, for the safety of our students and staff, we are no longer allowing her on school property. We strongly suggest you try homeschooling for a child with this many issues.

Sincerely,
Mrs. Zellet

OK, Mrs Zellet is a **LIAR!** Flushing that Hamster was NOT a accident!

My Sweet Miranda,

Welcome to your
new schoolbook!
I love you!
Love,
Mommy

i literaLy have
no idea wat
this says. you
have the worst handwriting in the worLd

Miranda
Age 8
3:00PM

Deer Mom,
it is NOT FARE that UR makeen me do HomeSkooLing. im ONLY 8 years OLd and forsing me too do stuF is aBuse i think. im 2 Busy 4 SKOOL anyWays. im trying to Brake the worLd record 4 how Long someone can hold a Little Bit oF dirt, and also my eLbow is relly ichy today so i CANT DO SKOOL! DONT EVER TALK TO ME again! Love, Miranda

my dum sister ruined my eitchurl!!

P.S. can we have tater tots 4 dinner?

My Sweet Miranda,

I made a fun worksheet for you today! Please finish spelling the words by filling in the blanks.

I love you!

-Mommy

Hi Mom.
2
This is
DUM!
Hahahahahaha!
A+++
very creative! A+++++ I love you! Love, mommy

My Sweet Miranda,

Today I think we need to work on something called "Manners". Please finish each sentence with something kind. Love, Mommy

EXAMPLE:

May I please have a hug?

Now You Try! ♡

Please Stop talking.
Excuse me, You Smell Like a Fart.
Thank you for Literly Nothing
I'm sorry your So anoying
I love Me.

A+++ great effort, sweetie!

My Sweet Miranda,

Please practice writing your name within the lines like this-

Miranda Miranda Miranda

Miranda Miranda

Miranda Miranda Miranda

This is impossibll!

Miranda Miranda

~~Miran~~ miranda Miranda Mira nada.

The Lines Keep moving!

NOT FAIR!

I know it's difficult, Keep trying!
I love you!

good News mom! i
Figurd out a easy
way to write in the
Lines. just cover them up!

Miranda Miranda
miranda miranda
Miranda. Miranda
Miranba Miranda
Miranda miranda Miran
Miranda Miranda
Miranda
Miranda

A+++

great work
sweetie! A+++!

Picture Day

Great job at your First homeschool picture day! Congrats on winning Most Photogenic in the whole school! I'm so proud of you sweetie!

A+++++! A++

See? I told you home schooling would be fun! Love, Mommy

UNCLE Jim is a grate Photogafer. That dum doll was anoying tho. i want Fish stiks

okay sweetie!

My Sweet Miranda,

Today we are learning about ADJECTIVES. An adjective is a word that describes something.

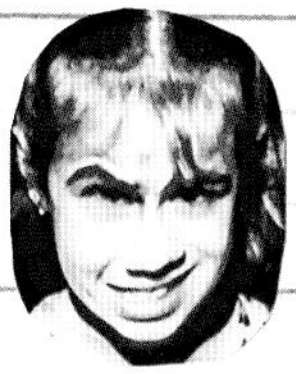

Example:

Miranda is beautiful!

Now you try!

Miranda is Me

Miranda is Me

Miranda is Me

Miranda is Choking a cat.

None of those words are adjectives, but you did get all of the answers right. A++++!

My Sweet Miranda,
Today I would really like you to try some math pretty please. I've made you a huge trophy for when you finish. I love you!
love, Mommy

1+1=	i
1+2=	am
1+3=	relly
1+4=	hungry
1+5=	BY.

No ofense But i will Never need to No this. its Been proven You dont use math in Life

Mommy + Miranda = ~~lots of love~~!

your a pervert.

you're right. I'm so sorry sweetie. I love you!

A+++

Miranda
Age 8, 2:01 pm

Dear Mom,
Please stop riting in my skool Book. Your hand riting is so slopy i can Barly reed it. its so Loopy. just tell me my skool and ill do it myself. also, How cum my sister has a ~~diarehee diarree diary~~ diarrhe and i dont? NOT FARE! So From now On this is my skool Book AND my diarrhe wich means its PRIVAT! You cant read it!

OK, sweetie. I understand. I'm sorry! I love you! A+++

Deer Diarrhe- Miranda Age 8
Mom said i need 2 pratice my cursive on this page Butt that is Boreen and i just got relly Busy cuz i got a posickle. i relly wanted a Froze toes Butt the Boy outside only had a rocket posickle. He gived me it free probly cuz he nos Im famus. That

Boy was relly werd and had ugly shoos and a Lout Like Butt i hope he cums Back tomorraw cuz i dont Like only seeing mom and my unkel every day. Also i want another posickle. That boy is nise Butt also I Like ise creem.

Love,

Miranda

my posicle stick

Miranda
Age 9 and 1/4

Dear Diarrhe,

grate news! i Fired mom
from Being my techer
today. She was always
telling me wat to do
during homskooling so i
was just like "Mom
stop talking or your
Fired" so then she sayd
"OK" and i was Like
"YOUR FIRED" and then
she cride. Butt now im my
own techer. so im proBLy
the First 9 years old
techer in the WORLD
im tired from riting this
so i need to tack a nap
OK By. Miranda

Dear Diarrhe, Miranda Age 9 and 1/3

My first day as a teacher went reLLY good. its very hard 2 Be a teacher AND a student so i made a skedule to Be orgdnize

skedule

12:00 - wake up
12:30 - eat Brekfast
1:00 - rest
1:30 - eat Lunch
2:00 - rest
3:00 - teach Miranda (me) skooL work
3:10 - eat snak
3:30 - pick that scaB
4:30 - rest
5:00 - eat snak
6:00 - eat dinner
7:00 - HomewoRK (wach TV)
8:00 - eat a Lot
Later - go to Bed

Today in SKOOL i teached myseLF a very importent Lessen. How to cut the eyes out of my Barbys

Dear Diarrhe,

Miranda
Age 7 and 3/4

i Found a ded Bird today. i took its Fethers to Play with. it was Fun.

PS.
i Put the Bird Body under moms Bed to play with Later.

Dear diarrhe, Miranda Age 9½

Today For skool i have decided to teach my self about my Favrite snaks and Practice eating them.

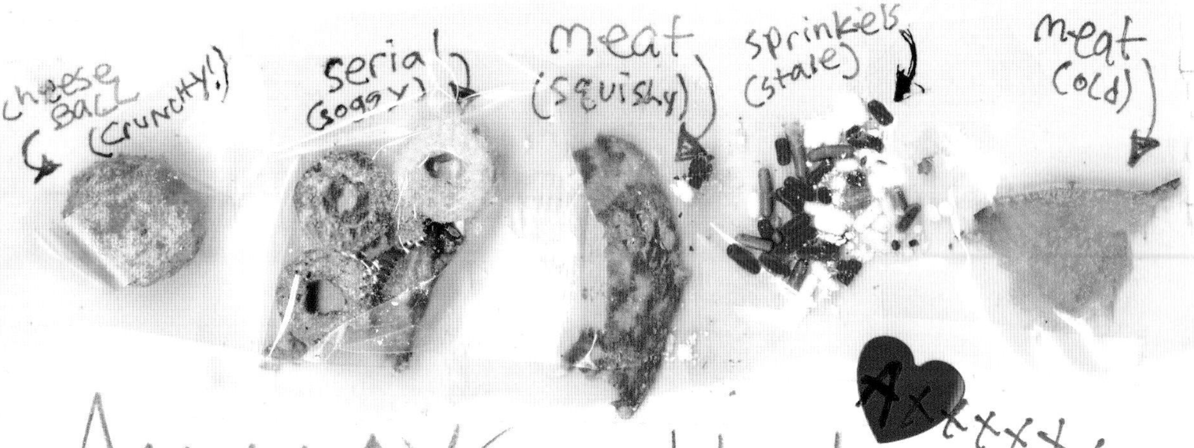

Anyways, that Boy with the posickles cummed over 2 my house

again today. i telled him we can only hang out if he dos everything i say. He sayd "it wuld Be my pleshur."

hes Wierd.

Anyways he has Been Bringeen me posickles for a lot of days and a lot of peepol are meen to him cuz hes a loser no ofense. Butt he Brings me

Posickle and he is
Nice so i gived him
My stuff aminal sloth
Hes my Best Frend.
Dont tell anybody tho
cuz hes relly wierd.

also i ate
Fish stiks
For Lunch
today. By.
Love
MIRANDA

Hes holdeen
a posickle in
case i drop
the 1 im holdeen

Dear Diarrhe,

miranda
Age 10
6:01 pm

Today for skool i decided to put on a HUGE Preformance of CATS

at the Park! i played all the parts and Uncle jim said i was so good and im gonna win a TONY! Butt im Not redy for a Boyfrend.

Anyways, after the show all the Boys were so impressed that they wouldnt Leave me alone.

← These Boys wanna Be with me so Bad they cant even keep there shirts on! wat a fun day.

♡ Miranda

me and my cousins

Deer Diarrhe,

miranda
Age who cares!

im haveen a **HORIBLE DAY!!!** First my Mom told me 2 get out of Bed wen i wasnt even redy and then my stupid Barby was staring at me!! DONT worry. i got her Back. Butt im sick of Being Disrespeted!!!

P.S. i didnt even have ANY eye crusties this morning! TOTAL RIPOFF! NOT

Love,
Miranda

Miranda
Age 10
3:07pm

Deer Diarrhe,
Today is a grate day! i decided im gonna Drop out of home skool and Focus on my modelling career! im so essited! My uncle said the 1st step is to make myself LOOK lick a model. So he put lots of pritty Lisstick on me just like models do AND gave me a Fancy Fur coat. i Look Amazeen!

MODEL! im never takeen off the listick!

So essited for this Netx chapter of my Life. im gonna Be FAMUS!

Diarrhe #3

Miranda's PRAYER JOURNAL

FOR GODS eyes ONLY!

miranda sings
Jan 2018
5:12PM

Diarrhe #3 is my prayer journaL from my pre pubeScent years. i was around 11-14 years old when i wrote in this. its a Fun one cuz i talk to God alot, Practise all my talents and Becum a mime.

However....
the end of this Diarrhe is relly Scary.
Beware.

Deer Diarrhe, miranda age 11

Mom gave me this journal to rite my prayers in and "get out my emotions". i dont have any of those Butt it would be good to write to God so i can aks him to give me wat i want. so im sorry diarrhe, Butt im gunna CALL you God, or Jesus, or hevenly Father, or Daddy in this journal so i can get my prayers ansered easier. OK, so. Hi God. PLease make mom give me that scooter. Thanks. in jesus name

GOODBYE,
miranda

P.S. Today i ate French fries and Lasania.

↑ in case you were wondering this is what i look like today.

Praise the Lord

Dear Jesus, miranda Age 11

we need 2 talk. i took AMAZING model shots at the department store last week with uncle jim and every day i look for my pitchurs on the cover of magizeens and its STILL NOT THEIR!?!! Not gunna lie... im relly frustrated with you God. i have been praying that you will make me famus for WEEKS and it still hasnt happened! i dont know why your ignoring me so tomorow im gonna go to church and aks you in person. you cant hide from me 4ever...

in Jesus name,
miranda

P.S. i had corn dogs 4 lunch

Praise the Lord

Hear are my model shots... so stunning.
i Like how you can see my scalp here.
im not a regular girL... im a cooL girL.
i call this pose "clenching it in."
me doing the splits
Praise the Lord

Dear Jesus, Miranda Age 11

So as you no i went 2 church today and mom **FORSED ME** to go 2 Sunday Skool. Their was a Bunch of girls waring Pink WWJD Braslets and i relly wanted 1 so i said "**Give me that Braslet! God sayd you HAVE TO or ELSE!**" and she didn't even do it!!!

see? Thats one of the mean girls with the Braslet.

So you need 2 punish her. Thanks. **ANYWAYS**, then i realized if i was Famus, i culd have all the WWJD Braslets i want! So i started Praying relly relly hard to Becum more Famus right away

Praise the Lord

and suddenly, out of nowhere, a old man who smells like lettuce started passing out these flyers to everyone at church!!

THIS WEEK AT CHURCH

AUDITION FOR A HOLLYWOOD MOVIE!

Tonight - 6 PM - Casting Call!

Pastor Mike wrote a movie called "Drummer Boy!" and he is looking for kids to audition for the shepherd children. The movie will premiere on our local public access channel on Christmas Day.

Monday - Single's Night

Let Jesus introduce you to your future soulmate!

Wednesday - Youth group

Hey Teens! You know what's cooler than drugs? Our Heavenly Father! Come get addicted to your new best friend. Jesus is dope!

Friday - Mime class

Taking a vow of silence? BORING! Make it fun and become a mime! Preach the Word without saying a word!

Finally! you gave me the anser to my prayers and showed me a way to get relly Famus!

Im going to Becum a mime!

Thanks 4 ansering my prayers.
in Jesus name,
miranda

Praise the Lord

P.S. Today i ate 3 cupcakes and a hot dog.

miranda
Age 12

Dear Heavenly Father,
that seems relly offichal.
can i just call you Daddy?
ill call you daddy.
Dear Daddy,
sorry we havnt talked in a
while, I Became a mime and
mimes arent aloud to talk.
at first i thought Being a
mime wuld help my modelling
career Becuz i thought it
stood 4 Models In Makeup Everywhere.

Praise the Lord

Butt it turns out Being a mime
just means your trapped in
a invisible Box a Lot. And
i need to think **OUTSIDE**
the Box. Plus those mime kids
Were relly wierd. So...
i Love you daddy Butt your
idea to get me Famus through
miming was WAY OFF. im
Loosing my pashense, and im
gonna ask you this one last
time. **God-Please Make me FAMUS!**
Rite NOW or else!
thank you.
Amen,
Miranda

P.S. if i dont wake up Famus i swear to God...
P.S.S. i ate MAC and cheese with tuna
and hot dog sLices for dinner.

Praise the Lord

Dear Daddy, miranda age 12

OK God, i have good news and Bad news. BAD NEWS?
i woke up NOT famus.
i asked you for ONE THING god.
ONE LITTLE THING!

see? this is what a NOT Famus Person Looks like

i told Mom and Uncle Jim that you didnt make me Famus yet and Mom said, "Have pashense." Butt she knows Nothing. Uncle Jim was SHOCKED. He said you Blessed me with so many talents that you oBviusLy WANT me 2 Be Famus so why hasnt it happend yet?!
so hear is the GOOD NEWS---
Uncle jim is gonna Be my Manager! Now im for sure gonna get Famus relly Fast! SCORE! in JESUS name,

Miranda.

AMEN

P.S. i wuld Like to pray for my hangNaiL it relly hurts.
P.SS. Uncle Jim asked me to pray that his Lactos intolerens goes away cuz he had ice cream and he doesnt want diary-Ah.
P.SSS. i had ice cream and Fried chicken today.

Praise the Lord

Dear Jesus Daddy, miranda Age 12

Grate News! My ~~uncle~~ Manager is working relly hard to get me Famus. First order of Busness? Make a List of all my talents so my ~~uncle~~ Manager no's what hes working with...

My List of talents
- singing
- dancing
- acting
- modeling
- eating
- talking
- Looking
- sLeeping
- Picking
- itching
- drinking
- snacking
- craft making
- whinning
- Being pretty
- Burning things
- T.V. watching
- staring
- teching
- Lerning
- Jumping
- walking
- Living
- other

He said he can work with this Butt my talents onLy count if the world sees them. so we snuck into my naybors house and i performed a original song i wrote called, "im Better then you." it was a hit! in Jesus Name,

me. miranda.

me singing
They Love me.
his jaw dropped cuz im so good

Praise the Lord

P.S. i ate chicken tenders and ice cream and salami for dinner.

Dear God,

miranda
age 12

i have **a LOT** of prayer requests today. im having a **HORRIBOL DAY!** i went to church and i saw those girls with the **WWJD** Braslets. i told them that im Famus now and i have a manager and every-thing and they **STILL** wuldnt give me there WWJD Braslets! **What the heck!!!** i even wore my Fanciest pink Dress that mom made me cuz it maches the Braslet perfeckly!!! i thought...

ugh! my mom just came in my room WITHOUT nocking and then she left without closing the door behind her, wich im pretty sure is ilegal. See what i mean? horibol day. so here are my prayer requests...

- PUNish Courtney.
- give me her Braslet.
- get me Famus Faster.
- make my mom stop being anoying.
- French Frys For Dinner.

AMEN.

♡ miranda

This is wat the Braslet looks like

Praise the Lord

Dear Daddy,

Miranda
Age 12

Thank you lord for giving me a GRATE DAY today. i am so Blessed. My ~~uncle~~ manager decided the next step to get me RELLY FAMUS wuld Be to get epic new Headshots, wich is Grate Becuz i have a LOT of audishons cuming up. West Side Story, Grease, Wizard of oz, Spice girls the musical, etc. my ~~uncle~~ manager said the only way ill get the lead in all those shows is if i have headshots that stand out and proove im Better then any1 else. How do we do that?

ELEPHANTS.

elephants are the Biggest, most epic, most Famus animol in the world.

"You are the company you keep" - God i think

So if i have a elephant in my headshot, it prooves im the Biggest, most epic, most Famus person in the world. So we went to the zoo, and got the most incredibol HeadSHOT in the WORLD!

Praise the Lord

Miranda

see? incrediBol. i hope i get in all the musicals! ♡ Miranda

P.S. Today i ate pizza cuz im trying to Be healthier.

Praise the Lord

Dear God, Miranda
Age 12

Grate News! The head shot worked! i got the lead in every single Play! Mom said they were the best homeskool plays we have ever done in the Living room! Thanks God. ♡ Miranda
Amen.

"Pray about it and youll get Famus." - The Bible Probly

P.S. Today i ate sausege.

Praise the Lord

Dear Jesus, Miranda Age 13
i went to church today and did this worksheet in sunday school

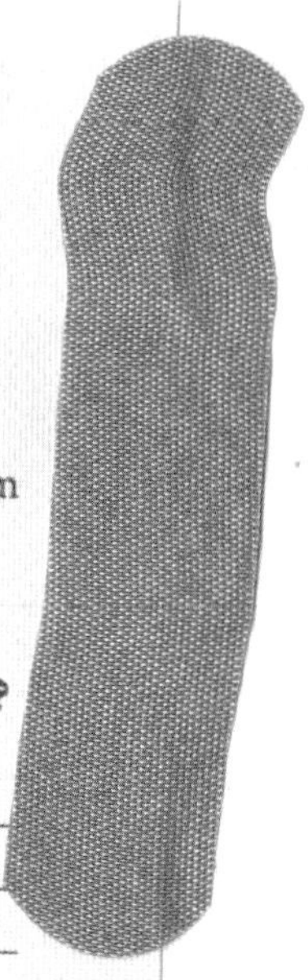

Faith

"For God so loved the world, that he gave his only Son, that whoever believes in him should not perish but have eternal life."
John 3:16

When was a time that you gave up something important for someone else?

One Time i gave up on school For myself cuz it was Boring.

"I can do all things through Christ who strengthens me"
Philippians 4:13

What does God give YOU the strength to do?

God gives me strength to rip my Barbys heads off even when they are on relly good. He also gives my ingrown toenail strength to keep growing Back.

"Love is patient, love is kind."
1 Corinthians 13:4

Who do you love enough to remain patient and kind for?

me.

its Been a while since i wrote to you cuz i have Been VERY Busy! Hear are all the things i have Been doing.

- My nayBor went on vacashon.
- i Lit a candel and took a Bath.
- i Burnt my hair on a candle.
- i stepped on a snail.
- i ate a Lot.
- i got a new Beanie Baby.
- i stepped on a very sharp crumb
- i ate aLot.

Butt i wanted to write to you cuz its Been MONTHS and im still not on the cover of ANY magazeens and im NOT super famus even tho ive aksed you a million times Butt i no im supposed to Be famus cuz look at me

So i think i no what the pRoBLem is, and i have Figured out a soLushon. Your not redy to anser my prayers cuz im not taking my relashonship with you serius enough...

Praise the Lord so....

We're getting married!

HusBands have to do whatever there wives want, so if we are married, you HAVE to make me Famus. Girls at church are always saying "im dating Jesus!" well im Marrying you. so stop dating those girls and make me Famus. also pay the Bills.

love, Your wife.

Praise the Lord

P.S. i ate a potato, grilled cheese, and chips today.

Dear Husband,

Miranda
Age 13

i have horribol news. i need to get a divorce. Mom said im not allowed to get married til im 21! Such a Rip off. So im sorry to brake your heart, Butt i have no choice. Today has Been so Bad. i cant Stop crying. Mom sayd she thinks im going thru puberty cuz im emochonal, irrashonal, and moody. Butt i dont no what shes talking about.

Me earlier today.

NOT LOVE,
miranda.

P.S. i ate ice cream, popcorn, and roast Beef casserole today.

Praise the Lord

Lord Forgive me 4 i have sinned. i said a Bad word on accident. i hired my BFF Patrick to Be my assistent Butt then realized theres a Bad word in his job title. i was tricked into saying it! Forgive me. it turns out theres a Lot of words that trick people to cuss, so i changed the names to help people to stop sinning.

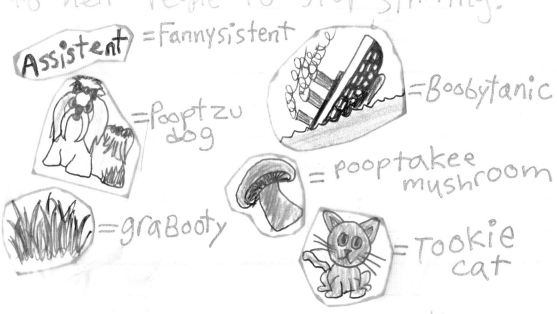

Assistent =Fannysistent

=Pooptzu dog

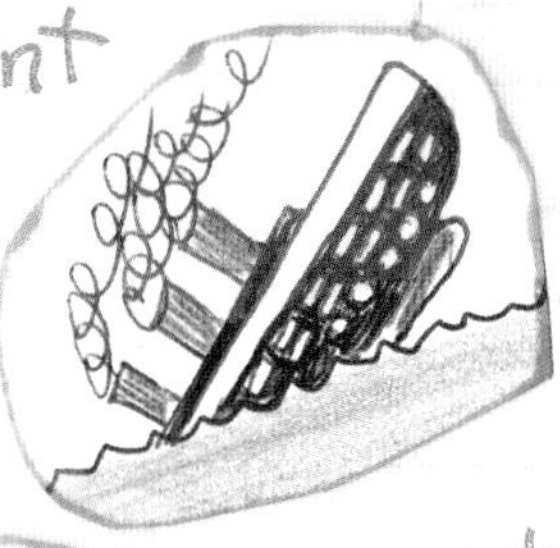
=Boobytanic

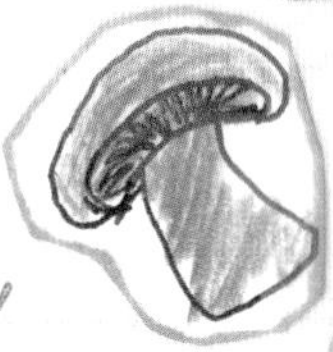
=pooptakee mushroom

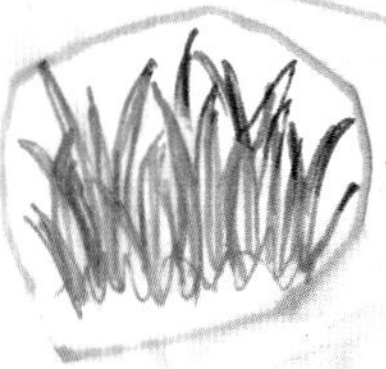
=graBooty

=Tookie cat

Let me no if their are other words you need me to change 4 you God. Forgive me. i Love u. Amen,

Miranda

P.S. i ate Bacon, popsicles, pickles, and Lunch meat today.

Praise the Lord

Dear Jesus, age 13

i have a very importent prayer today. i need you to punish my Mommy relly Bad. she made me get Brases and they hurt SO BAD! This is child abuse FOR SURE! I called the cops and they didnt even arrest her. so my prayer 2day is that you arrest her and tech her a Lesson 4 abusing me! ALSO, i want the prinsess diana Beanie Baby. And i want to Be Famus.

Love,
Miranda AMEN

p.s. i ate tator tots and cupcakes today. and some chees Balls.

Brases are DUMB! I hate this!

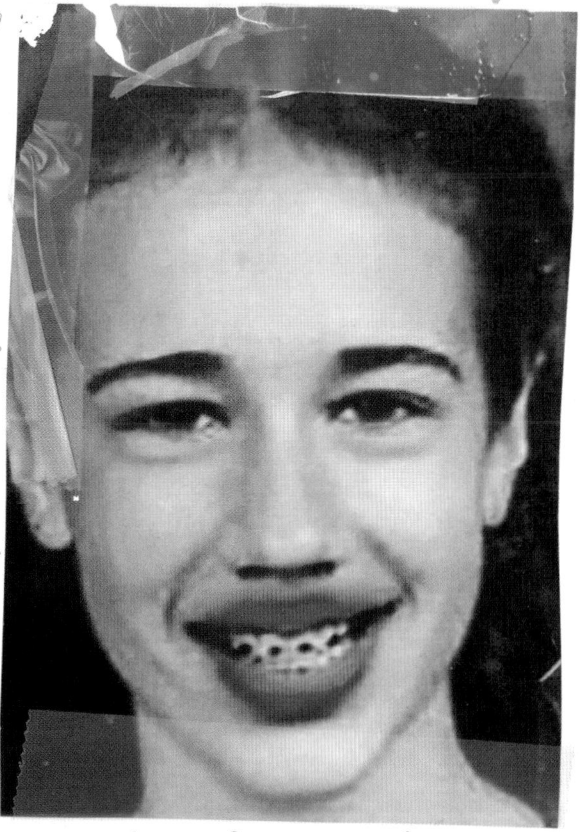

im smiling in this pic Butt dont be Fooled. im crying inside.

Praise the Lord

Dear Jesus,   Age 13

Thank you 4 ansering my Prayers. Mom slipped on a pile of my toys and broke her Finger so she definitly lernd her Lesson For giving me these Braces. i also noticed shes getting a Bald spot. You always go above and beyond to please me, Lord. That was a nice tuch. Thank you. My uncle took me to get model pics at sears, and im starteen to like my Braces. Plus the rubber Bands are Fun to save. some times they have food still on them. im going to save them all. Thank you Lord. i am Blessed. Love,

Miranda

AMEN

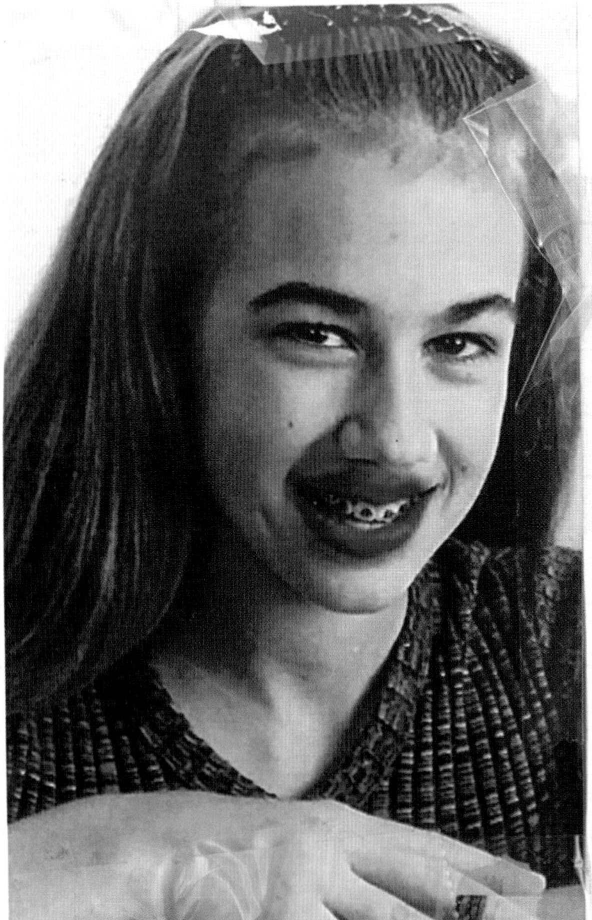

P.S. Today i ate 3 chees Burgers. Praise the Lord

Dear Lord, Miranda Age 13

Today at church the girls with the WWJD Braslets called me Brase Face. i am so exsited they gave me a cute Nick Name. i think it means im there frend now and they will give me a Braslet to mach theres! FINALLY! i new you would anser my prayers! Butt mom is Being a total Hater. On the way home from church she said, "Those girls are not your frends!". Shes' so jelus of me!! i told her i need one of those Braslets Butt she just dosn't understand. its not fare they all have 1 and i dont.

Whatever. Mom cant upset me today. My ~~uncle~~ manager borrowd $500 from moms savings and got me fancy profeshonal model pitchurs from a REAL Photografer! Hes gonna send them to all the magazeens to get me on a cover and get me FAMUS! the pitchurs turned out Grate! →

Praise the Lord

see? They R so good.

This photo shows off my FlexaBility

This photo shows how popular I am. Look at all my friends.

Another friend. i named her jim Toots.

This photo shows how much i hate PLants

This photo shows off my sitting talent

This photo shows im a sofisticated model that always Knows what time it is.

Amen,
Miranda

P.S. i ate corn and ground Beef today.

Dear Diarrhe, miranda Age 13 4:27 pm

THIS IS THE BEST DAY EVER! mom said we are gonna go to a New church cuz im 2 Famus 4 the old one. Butt she told me those girls gave her a WWJD BrasLet for me! FINALLY! They told her that they Love me and think im too amazing 4 them. i agree.

Anyways, it Looks a Lot diferent From there BrasLets Butt it maches the dress Mom made me perfeckly! Literaly the same materiel and everything! im so Happy! Also my ~~uncle~~ manager sent my model shots to all the movies and TV shows and models so ill proBLy get super Famus any day now. Nothing can go wrong! My LIFE is PERFECT!

♡ miranda

Praise the Lord

P.S. today i ate tons of meat and also hot dogs.

God—

My Period started.

How could you do this to me?!

My Life is

OVER!

Bye.

~~Praise the Lord~~

My life is over!

Diarrhe #4
MSG
other?
daydream
KEEP OUT!
SCHOOL
Edgy
rude"
kiss
Pizza
Top Secret!!!
parents
hottie
Monster
DONT READ
UNLESS you want me to kick ur BUTT
Whaterer!
Expires
ALRIGHT!
speak my mind!
GO AWAY!
to
CRUSH
f Your
ed. Keep out of reach of children.
Chow Fun 炒粉類

Miranda Sings
Jan 2, 2018
5:49 pm

Diarrhe#4 is

the journal i kept during my teenage years. its **VERY** emotchonal so Be prepared to cry. i had my First kiss, my first heartBrake, and my First viral video that changed [redacted] my Life Forever...

♡ miranda

Dear Diarrhe,
Miranda
age 13

my real tear drops!

This is the worst day of my Life! i almost Died. i was too upset before to tell you the story but now i have this new jurnal and ive calmed down. Basicly my tummy was hurting and i thot it was cuz i added too much kechup to moms cheesBall tuna casserole so i went to the Bathroom, to get it out. all the sodden there was Blood in the Potty! i started screaming "IVE BEEN SHOT!" my mom came in and said its just a period and she got hers when she was 13 too. SHE DID this to ME! SHE GAVE ME THIS DISEESE! i WILL NEVER FORGIVE HER FOR THIS! My tummy hurts. My diaper iches. im running away From home. BYE.

NOT LOVE,
Miranda

Dear Diarrhe, miranda Age14, 5:13pm

ive decided to put my career on hold. Obviusly i want to Be Famus Butt i just have 2 many emotchons rite now. i cant handle the stress of Fame <u>and</u> try to deal with Becumming a woman. STOP pressuring ME!! i wrote some poetry on My napkins at the taco place and i think they relly show my Feelings good.

Love, Miranda

Roses are Red
viLets are BLue
i hate everyone.

Dear Everyone,
go away.
Love,
Miranda.

i never get anything i want
Their is Blood cumming from my Front.
i relly dont like anyone,
that includes your son.
No one cares aBout me,
its annoying when i have 2 pee.
(in the middle of the nite)
Life is totally unFair
i like steak medium rare.
My mommy is the dumBest
At Least i have BuBBLegum...
est.

Dear Diarrhe, Miranda Sings Age14, 8:21pm

UGH! Why do Bad things always happen to good people?! Today is AWFUL! im just trying to Be a good American sitizen and Live my Best Life, Butt so many Terrible things Keep happening to me that usually onLy happen in hell PROBLY.

i poured a Bowl of cereal and their was NO MILK!

i was squirting my ketchup and a Bunch of that Poisen ketchup water came out first and ruined every thing

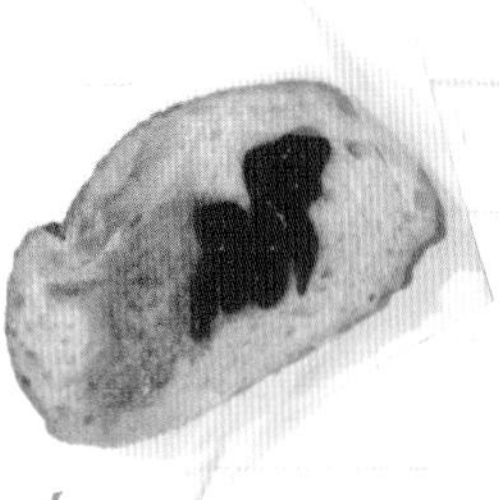

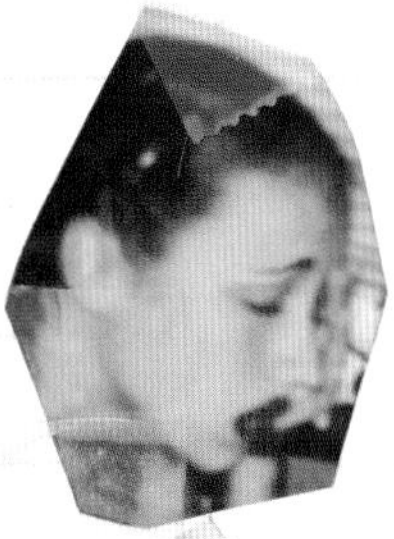

my mom talked to me

i had to sneeze relly Bad and then it disapeared. Rip off!

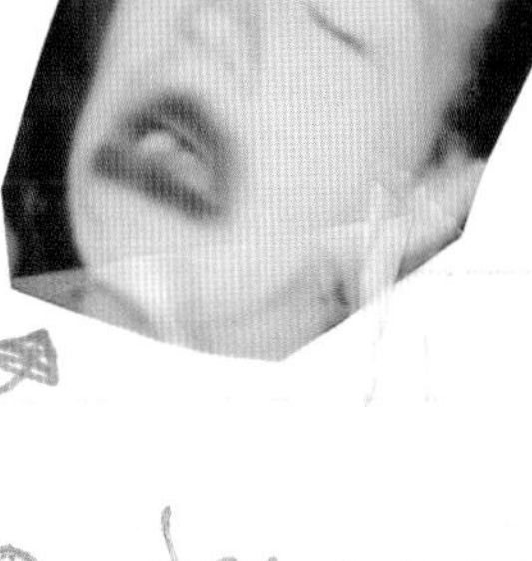

i stuBBed my toe relly hard.

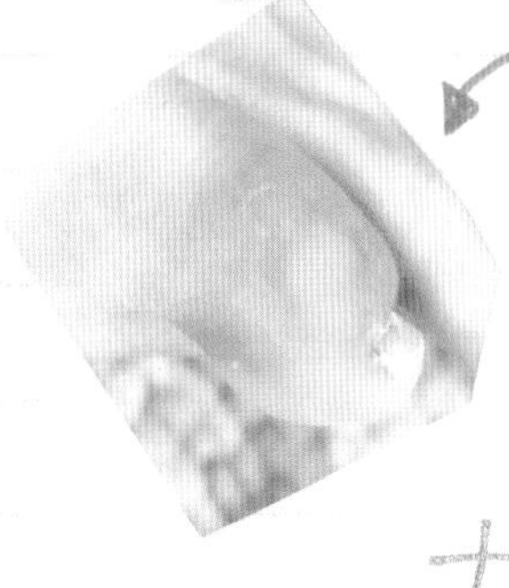

what did i do to deserve all of these Satanic things? My Life is so UNFARE! Anyways, gotta go! We are going to the movies and getting ice cream! Yay! Bye. ♡ Miranda

Dear Diarrhe,

Miranda
Age 16

As you know, everything has Been totaly UNFAIR in my Life Lately. My mom always wakes me up BEFORE my alarm, Barley any1 knows im Famus still, every1 is annoying, and i hate everything. **BUTT** things are finally Looking up FOR ONCE IN MY LIFE! i have huge News! Are you redy for it? i have... A BOYFREND! My First Boyfrend! Can you Beleve it?!? Hes relly cute and His name is Michael! We have Ben going to the same church for a while Butt this Sunday he made it offishal! HE SAT NEXT TO ME AND HELD MY HAND! Your only suposed to do that with your wife so. Things are moving relly Fast. And honestly i think he would have done it even if the paster didnt say "Lets all hold hands for prayer." He pulled his hand away half way thru the prayer and his hand was pretty Limp Butt i think he was trying to Be respecFuL since we arnt married yet. ALSO my hand was pretty wet so he proBLy relly Loved that and didnt want 2 Lust over me. Oh! and get this! he's aLSo my SUGAR DADDY! He gave me $$$! They passed around a [redacted] donate PLate at church and he put 5 dollers in it, handed me the pLate and SMILED! im not Dum, i no what that means. So i took the 5$$ and winked at him relly hard. Then he moved seats.

i HAVE A BOYFREND! i cant wait til church on Sun day so i can see him again! i Love him!

Dear Diarrhe,

Miranda
Age 16

my relashonship with Michael is going relly good. Every day this week i went to his house when he was at school to get to know him Better. ive learned that he likes the spice girls, cheetos, and the organ trail. i got on his computer yesterday and tried to win it 4 him as a suprise Butt i acsidentally died of dysentary.

He must know im cumming everyday cuz he leaves the window unloked For me. Hes so thotful. i gave him this letter

at Church on sunday and he opened it and then gave it Back and walked away. i literaly left him speechless! i Love him so much! i cant wait till we are married!

Miranda

2 my BOYFREND michael ~

Thanks 4 makeen our relashonship offishal By Holding my Hand at church Last week. Sorry i killed you of Dysentary. i hope your not mad. iF you are thats relly imature cuz i was just trying 2 help so u better stop Being mad RITE NOW. is this our First Fight?!? Your Being a JERK. im sorry. i hate wen we fight. i love you.

ANYWAYS, i just wanted to say even tho im hotter and more Famus then you, i think this can work, even tho i'm WAY out of your Leeg. Your SO LUCKY. Do you like this cat? i took him from my neighBors Back yard and every nite i put flowers on him in Bed and pretend its you. Butt dont worry! Tonite i'll come to your house and do it to you insted of the cat. i cant wait! i LOVE YOU! Cant wait 2 spend the rest of my life with you! Love YOU.

miranda

PS. if i ever see you with another girl your dead meat.

Miranda Sings
2:13 P.M.

Dear Diarrhe,

ok, so Michael is playing hard to get and its relly annoying. i get that this is just his way of Flirting Butt its gonna Be hard for our relashonship to grow if he Keeps running away from me, and Locking his doors and windows so i cant get in his house. At church the other day i gave him a Bag of relly thotFull presents and he handed it Back and ran away. Hes so sweet. He new how much i wuld love all the stuFF in the Bag so he wanted me 2 have it.

Miranda

P.S. ValentimeS day is cumming up and he Better propose!

Miranda Sings
7:42 pm

Dear Diarrhe,

i am HartBroken!!! i had 2 Brake up with Michael today. i went to his house today and he was packing things into a truck. This is the hartBraking conversashon we had-

Michael-"i can see you in the Bushes. Please stop."

Me-"where are you going?"

Michael-"im moving"

Me-"Your Leaving me???"

Michael-"Yes. We are moving 2 Utah"

Me-"i cant Beleve your Braking up with me."

Michael-"im Not your BoyFrend!"

Me-"i know! Cuz we just Broke up you jerk! You dont have 2 rub it in! Fine! iM Braking up with YOU!! **its over!**"

Hes Being a Total Brat Butt i no he loves me. Valentimes day is next week so im sure he will apologize and we will Live hapilly ever after. i love him so much.

Miranda

BYE
NOT REEL
Valentine's Day
14
FAKE
NOT
STU
DUM
HATE

Dear Dum Diarrhe, Miranda Age WhO CARES

ValentiMes Day is **SO DUM!** People who arnt in a relashonship are reminded aLL day that they R aLone 4EVER and people who Do have a relashonship stress about makeen the day Perfekt. its a Loose Loose situashon!!!!! i dont even care that im single on valentimes day. **Stop saying that i care cuz i DONT! i dont care** that Michael wont call me Back. **i dont care** that he didnt give me a valentime or say thank you 4 the one i gave him. **i DONT CARE! im going to BE ALONE FOREVER AND i DONT CARE!!** The ONLY reason i got Mad today is cuz i TOOK a Bite out of one of the chocoLates mom gave me and it had a freaking cherry in it! i might as well eat **POISEN** cuz its the **same thing!** Fruit has NO PLACE Near chocolate! **VaLentimes Day is RUINED!** i wiLL **Never seleBrate this HoLiday!** I **HATE IT!!!!**

(unless Michael asks me out. that wuld Be so cuuute! ♡♡)

NOT Love, Miranda

Dear Diarrhe,

Miranda Sings
2:13 pm

my dum mom is FORSING ME to do chores. This is Child ABUSE! Well jokes on her cuz when i was dusting i Found dust. $Cha Ching!$ im gonna Be a million nair. im gonna make my own Line oF dust stuffed aminals, sell them, get RICH and move out! Then mom will miss me so much and regret Forsing me to do chores. Best revenge ever!

im gonna make a Forchune!

♡ Miranda

Miranda Sings Age

Dear Diarrhe,

oh my gosh!! Today i had my **First Kiss** Finally! it was so amazing and super fun! i was relly nervus cuz i had never done it Before Butt it was Better than i culd have imagined. **AND** — it was a French Kiss! can you Beleve it? OK, so hear is the story—

OBviusly things didnt work out with Michael Butt i Knew i was redy 4 my First Kiss anyway. So... i sat down on my Bed, and kissed My Knee. i did it For Like 5 minutes. it was relly romantic and tasted Like cheese Balls wich was a Big Bonus. i am on cloud 9! im in LOVE!

Miranda

Dear Diarrhe, Miranda

sorry i havent written in hear in so Long! its Been Years! Butt ive BEEN BUSY GET OFF MY BACK!!! Lets see... what have i Been up too... i got a Pink Jacket, i Found a new Brand of hot dog i relly like and my career is about to explode. Uncle jim got a video camera so we can uplode videos of me to the interntet and show the world my talents. i guess their is a website called YouTube that he wants 2 use. We are gonna film the first one today. Oh! ALSO—i have a relly good scab Forming. Gotta go. Uncle jim wants to film this video. ♡

Miranda

my new jacket!

my new favorit hot dogs

Dear Diarrhe,

Miranda Sings
April 2009

a **LOT** has happened. We uploded that video and it got a **TON** of views, Like **49!** My uncle came up with this 5 phase PLan to get me Famus. We are hafway thru the Fazes so i shuld Be Famus pretty soon. i did a Big Preformence in the Big Attle (seattle) and my uncle let me Borrow his **red swetpants.** They feel good in all the creeses so im gunna start waring them all the time. THEN we did **ANNIE** in the BackYard. Butt it got ruined cuz some1 clogged the toilet. Patrick played Daddy WarBux and i played annie and something weird happened. i felt relly gassy and Floaty when we did the romantic scene. ANYWAYS i gotta go Becum a Magichan. ♡

Miranda

p.s. im the one who clogged the toilet.

miranda April 2009
6:12 PM

Dear Diarrhe,

Uncle Jim is relly anoying me. his dumb 5 Faze plan to get me Famus **is** taking **FOR EVER** so im just gonna get myself Famus on my own. i dont no how yet Butt ill Figure it out. i shuld Be the **MOST Famus person in the world** By now! **ugh!** Being me is relly hard. **and** to make matters worser, Uncle Jim keeps talking about uploding a video that i **DONT** want him 2 post. its called **"Free voice Lesson"** and it gives away **ALL** my Singing secrets! hes such a idiot.

Anyways, i didnt poop yet today so at lesf i have that to look forward to. gotta go. Full house is on. BY.

♡ Miranda

Dear Diarrhe,

miranda
April 2009
9:02 pm

Uncle Jim uploaded that video.

it went viral.

obsessed
TOP
Secret!
Whoa!
crush
Silly
CUTIE
Dreaming of my boy!
TOP
Tuck!
Hot
SHY

miranda
Diarrhe#5
2009
2009
Private!
ONLY UNCLE
jim can read!

Miranda Sings
Jan 2, 2018
6:02 pm

Diarrhe #5

is the journal i kept rite aFter i got my first viral video. i was roBBed, Cheated, and Disrespeted. Butt i never stopped Begging people to give me money and make me Famuser.

#NeverGiveUp
#ImAnInspirashon

Miranda Sings
May 1, 2009
2:07 PM

Dear Diarrhe,

a **LOT** has happened since i last wrote to you so i decided to get a new diarrhe. Hear is every thing that happened since we last talked:

- i got famus
- i got a Boyfrend
- my whole family and BF left me.
- i got them Back
- i ate a LOT of CheeseBalls
- went to NYC with my Dad.
- i got MORE Famouser
- my dad left. hes dumb.
- i came home to my Family
- i ate a popsicle
- a girl named Colen is impostering Me.
- we got evicted.
- i got a hangnail.

So thats what you missed. im Literaly so stressed. And to make matters worse, i stepped in a tiny puddle in the Bathroom in my **SOCKS**! Now i have a soggy toe. BYE! ♡, miranda

Dear Diarrhe,

miranda Sings
May 3, 2009, 3:29 pm

So uncle jim and me desided to go on a **WORLd tour!** we want to do it For 3 reasons –

1. cuz im Famus
2. to Find my imposter Colline
3. Frankie Grande (a guy i met in NYC) said i can always call him if i need anything at all.

So we are gonna tour to NYC, get me on Brodway, and make Frankie give me his apartment.

By the way, this is my imposter

Frankie and me last time i was in NYC. i gave him a voice lesson.

im way prettier then her.

her eyeBrows Look Like somthing i lerned aBout in healthclass

i can see her chestical crack! Porn!

Uncle Jim said we dont have any shows Booked for this tour yet Butt he's pretty sure if we just show up at venues they will let me preform. He's such a good Manager. OK time to go to our First show!

♡ miranda Sings

Miranda Sings
May 4, 2009 5:21PM

Dear Diarrhe,

im writing to you from inside
the Mini van on Tour! We are in
Portland now wich im pretty sure is
a diFFerent cuntry. All the people
hear seem foreign. They all have
Big mustashes, Lots of tattoos, they
only eat coffee, and they all want
to Be Farmers. im having culture
shock Butt Luckily im 1/8 Polish so i
understand the Language pretty good.
We tried to get on stage during a
comunity theater preformance OF OKLAHOMA
Butt we got Kicked out. We also got kicked
out of a "Liberals only coffee shop," a "animal free
circus," and 5 farmers markets for trying
to perform. TouR Life is so Fun!
ive Been uploading to YouTuBe aLOT
Lately! Hear are sum of my favrites-

"my fist music video Genie in a Bottle"

"single Ladies"

"im relly sick. spoon full of sugar"

"respect"

We just got to our next stop! Wish
me Luck! ♡ Miranda

Miranda Sings
May 2009
:59 PM

Dear Diarrhe,

Tour is going grate! We just finished our first show! This is a pitchur of the audience we had!

Those Ladies mite Look quiet Butt they were rowDy! in the middle of my opening number one of them yelled "BINGO!". She oBviusLy got my name wrong Butt i Forgave her after i kicked her out. WeLL, im exhausted and i have to [redacted] pee. Tour Life is crazy! Good Nite. Love,

Miranda

Dear Diarrhe,

Miranda Sings
May 2009 9:01 PM

Today i did a show in UTAH! Normaly we just show up at theaters and hope they Let us in Butt this time a guy called and said he wuld give me my very OWN SHOW at the Kids museum he works at! We snuck in after it closed. i asked if it was Legal and he said he turned off all the security alarms & cameras. i got to decide wich Kid area to perform in. i almost chose the kid size grosery store Butt i ended up picking the kid size oval office cuz im proBLy gonna Be precidenx soon. We sold 40 tickets at 30 dollers a pop! i dont no how much that adds up to cuz im not a scientist Butt my uncle says it over $1,000 so that means we are gonna Be MILLIONAIRS! ♡, Miranda

me performing in my oval office
The audiense got to sit on kid chairs.

Dear Diarrhe,

Miranda Sings
May 2009 2:49pm

UGH! that guy from Utah **STOLE OUR MONEY!** when we called him to get paid he said hes gonna keep all the money cuz he used a lot of gas driving to the museum 4 my show. i kinda understand cuz i herd gas is espensive Butt he shuld at lest give me a cupple dollers! Then he **Blocked** our phone # so we culdn't contact him anymore. **ugh!** Uncle jim says this is a good thing cuz now i have a scandal and when the news picks up the story ill get even more famuser.

ANYWAYS, we found a pretty chair in someones yard 2day and did a photo shoot with it. im gonna send a copy to santa to prove ive Been a good girl. im also gonna send a copy to that guy in Utah to tech him a lesson.

Bye.
miranda

ive Been a very **VERY** good girl... xoxo

For santa

For dumB Utah guy

i hope u get a deep paper cut.

Hi Diarrhe, Miranda Sings may? 2009 11:12 AM

we drove around for a **LONG TIME** today Looking For New York City. we dindt Find it Butt we ended up in **Sacamento, CA!** i thot sacamentos were just those red things inside green oLives, Butt it turns out its a city too. We found a choir concert at a school so i went on stage and decided they wuLd Be my Backup Singers. The choir conducter waches my videos so he didnt call the cops! it was my Best Preformance on tour so far!

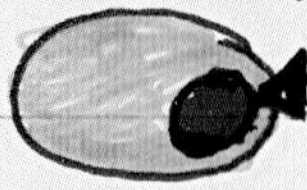

Bohemien Rapsidy

YMCA

The choir techer even Let us sleep at his house witch was nice cuz im sick of sLeeping in the car. HopFully we will make it to NYC soon, cuz this tour is getting relly hard. gotta go. i just found a ingrown hair and i relly wanna get it. Bye.

♡ Miranda

Miranda Sings
May 2009

Dear Diarrhe,

im not sure where we are Butt i think its the middle of nowhere. So mayBe Lompoc? Uncle jim rented out a theater for my show 2nite! it costed all the money we have Left Butt he is confident we will make the Money Back in ticket sales. So we are gonna go 2 the sizzler to pass out these Fliers to promote the show. →
Every1 loves Sizzler so i Bet my show will Be sold out! THINGS R LOOKING UP! NYC HEAR WE CUM! ♡

Miranda

SO YOU LIKE BUFFETS HUH?
THEN YOU'LL LOVE THE FAMus
MIRANDA SINGS FROM YOUTUBE!

PERFORMANCE TONIGHT!
ONE NIGHT ONLY!
the high school down the street. $5 per ticket

Miranda Sings
May 2009

Dear Diarrhe,

The show just ended. Only 10 old Ladies showed up. Butt i was doing the **Best Performence of my Life** so i dindt even care. The Feeling i felt on stage was **so amazing.** it Felt Better then the feeling of a Q-tip deep in your ear after a shower. Better then when you pick off a scaB in one peace and it doesnt even Bleed. Better then every Mary Kate & Ashly olsen movie comBined. **Butt then.....** something terriBLe happened. Every1 started walking out of the theater. **What the heck!** im Famus. How could this happen to me?! OLd Ladies who can Barely walk... **WALKED OUT OF MY SHOW in the Middle OF THE PREFORMENCE!** Well... tecknicly one rolled out in a wheelchair. and a couple of them scooted out on walkers... **Butt still!!! HATER!** They will regret it. just wait and see. im gunna proove those old **L**adies wrong. WOAH! a Big Bug just hit the windsheeld. That was proBLy God telling me im gonna get revenge on those Ladies. Thanks Big guy. You always got my Back.

♡ Miranda

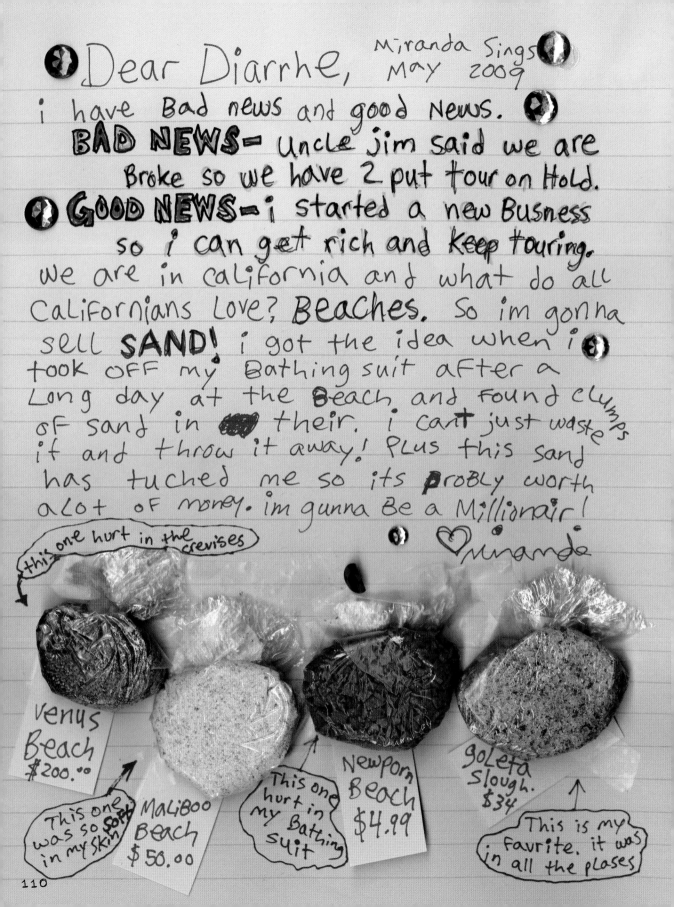

Miranda Sings
May 2009

Dear Diarrhe,

i have Bad news and good News.

BAD NEWS- Uncle jim said we are Broke so we have 2 put tour on Hold.

GOOD NEWS- i started a new Busness so i can get rich and Keep touring.

We are in california and what do all Californians Love? Beaches. So im gonna sell **SAND!** i got the idea when i took OFF my Bathing suit after a Long day at the Beach and found clumps of sand in [redacted] their. i cant just waste it and throw it away! PLus this sand has tuched me so its probLy worth alot of money. im gunna Be a Millionair!

♡ Miranda

this one hurt in the crevises
Venus Beach $200.00
This one was so soft in my skin
MaLiBoo Beach $50.00
This one hurt in my Bathing suit
Newporn Beach $4.99
goLeta Slough. $34
This is my favrite. it was in all the plases

Miranda Sings
May 2009 6:22 pm

Dear Diarrhe,

You will **NEVER BELEVE** all the stuff that happened 2day! **First** - a Big Producer said he wanted me to Be in "Guys & Dolls" on Broadway! so i met him in L.A. and he said i was casted! Butt then he said "Before rehersals, i want you to do a video with me and Let **ME** Be the one to reveel your true identity to the world! your real name is coalleen, rite?"

~~UGHHHHHHHHHHHHHH~~!!!!!!

i told him he can **NOT** do that and then he said i wasnt in the show anymore! what the heck! That dumB imposter is ruining my LiFe! **THEN** i got a call from a theater in Miami, Florida that wants to Book me! Butt i dont have money for a plane ticket so i dont know how im gonna get their. Good News is, i think Miami is next to NYC, so if i can get their i'll Be golden.

♡ Miranda

P.S. my sand Busness didnt work out. i only sold 1 Bag of sand.

P.S.S. my knee is VERY ichy today.

Hi Diarrhe,

Miranda Sings
May 2009 2:19 PM

i made it 2 **Miami**! it turns out the guy who Bought a Bag of sand From me is a **Big Fan** of my videos! His name is Ryan, and he asked me 2 sing at his Birthday Party at a gay CLUB in LA. and **GUESS WAT?!** He paide me! 200 dollers! it onLy paid for 1 Flight to Miami so i took it and Uncle jim stayed in California with my grandma. The show is **TONITE!** And then ill Be rich and Famus, go to NYC, tell Broadway to give me a show, make Frankie give me his apartment, Find my imposter and tell her to **BACK OFF**, and Live hapilly ever after. im so essited!

♥ miranda

me preforming at Ryans B Day party

THings are Finally working out!

Dear Diarrhe

Miranda Sings ♡
May 2009 10:01 PM

THings are NOT working OUT!!!

while i was performing on stage everything in my dressing room got **stoLen!** i didnt panick too much cuz i knew i was about to make a lot of Money From my show. Butt the theater manager said she didnt need to pay me cuz we didnt have a contract. **SO UNFAIR!** i cant help that God made me perfect with 20/20 vishon so i dont need **gLasses** or **contacts!** ripoff... **im sick of THis!** Ive Been on tour for ~~months~~ ~~weeks~~ days and ive delt with people rejecting me, ive Been sleeping in a car, i havent had <u>any</u> supersize fries—onLy regular, and now ive Been robbed. **i thot Famus PeopLe were supposed to have it easy and get everything they want!**

So i did what any sane person would do in my posishon. i called my rich, Famus frend and Begged him to give me money. After all, Frankie <u>DID</u> say "call me if you need anything at all!" ...i definitly need anything at all rite now. i hope he calls me Back soon cuz i relly need to pee.

♡ Miranda

Miranda Sings

Dear Diarrhe,

EVERYTHING worked out! iM Famus! i KNEW i was Famus! i KNEW i wuld proove those old Ladies wrong! idiots... SO... Frankie Grande ended up Flying me to NYC and he let me stay with him. He wuldnt give me his apartment wich i think is relly rude, Butt im thinking aBout changing the Locks next time hes not home.

ANYWAYS, ALOT has happened in the last couple weeks! iLL try to summ it up in the next couple of pages.

♡ Miranda

i performed with Frankie Grande alot in NYC. i think we r dating. i got relly close to his mom and sister while i was there too. im gonna start giving his sister Ariana voice Lessons. she relly needs my help.

i performed with the Brodway cast of Mama Mia at a Big Event. Someone Filmed the hole thing so if i ever wanna wach it again i can just scan this code. (P.S. i Blurred the faces of the people i didnt like.)

video of me and Mama Mia

video of me at Brodway on Brodway

This is Seth rudetskey. i never herd of him but hes famus and i met him when i snuck on stage at Brodway on Brodway in Time square

LONDON.

i went to LONDON! A produser said he could get me on stage in the west End. i didnt wanna go cuz "the west end" sounded like a gang and i dont like guns. Butt then he said the west end is like Brodway Butt for people with British accents. So i went and suddenly my experiense in the West end went SOUTH. Somehow i ended up on stage with the cast of "Naked Boys Singing". it was TRAMOTIZING! i spent the hole show trying to cover up their privases.

if anyone ever saw this it wuld RUIN my career.

Hopefully those are the Last naked Boys i will ever see. The rest of my trip to London was grate! i performed with TONS of People from the west end. (the singing and dancing kind. Not the gang kind.) So other then the naked nightmare, i Loved London. Somehow i understood every one perfectLy even though i dont speak British. i guess im just relly smart. ♡, Miranda

Some videos of my West End Preformenses

taking pics with fans at a gay Bar

me preforming at a school dance or something

me and the west end cast of Chicago ♥

i Flew Back to NYC after London and Preformed a Lot more! i gave the Brodway cast of "rock of ages" a voice Lesson cuz they needed it relly Bad. Hears the video from it.

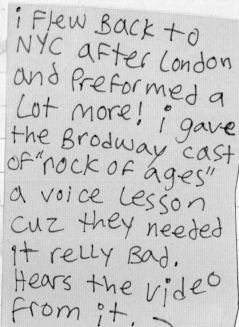

i Performed at Jim Caruso's cast Party. Jim said i can do my own 1 women show at BirdLand jazz cLUB whenever i want. He said im gonna Be a STAR! oh and this is some anoying girL i performed with.

And last Butt not Least, i Found that dum imposter, **Coalleen**. She said shes not gonna stop impostering me cuz it gets her views. She's so OBsessed with me! So we decided to make a deal. i cant tell you what it is cuz its TOP SECRET and i wuld have to kill you, Butt we made a video together. im pretty sure i dont have to worry about her cuz shes kinda ugly and not talented (no offense) so she will never get Famus. its proBLy the Last time i will ever hear about her to Be honest.

This is the video we did together. She is not good.

ANYWAYS, im Back home in Tacoma now. its Been a crazy month, Butt im so glad everyone Finally knows im Famus. From Now on, ill Be living a classy, Fancy life Full of Glitz and Glamer!!! Gotta go... uncle jim is clipping his toe nails and i like to watch.

♡ miranda

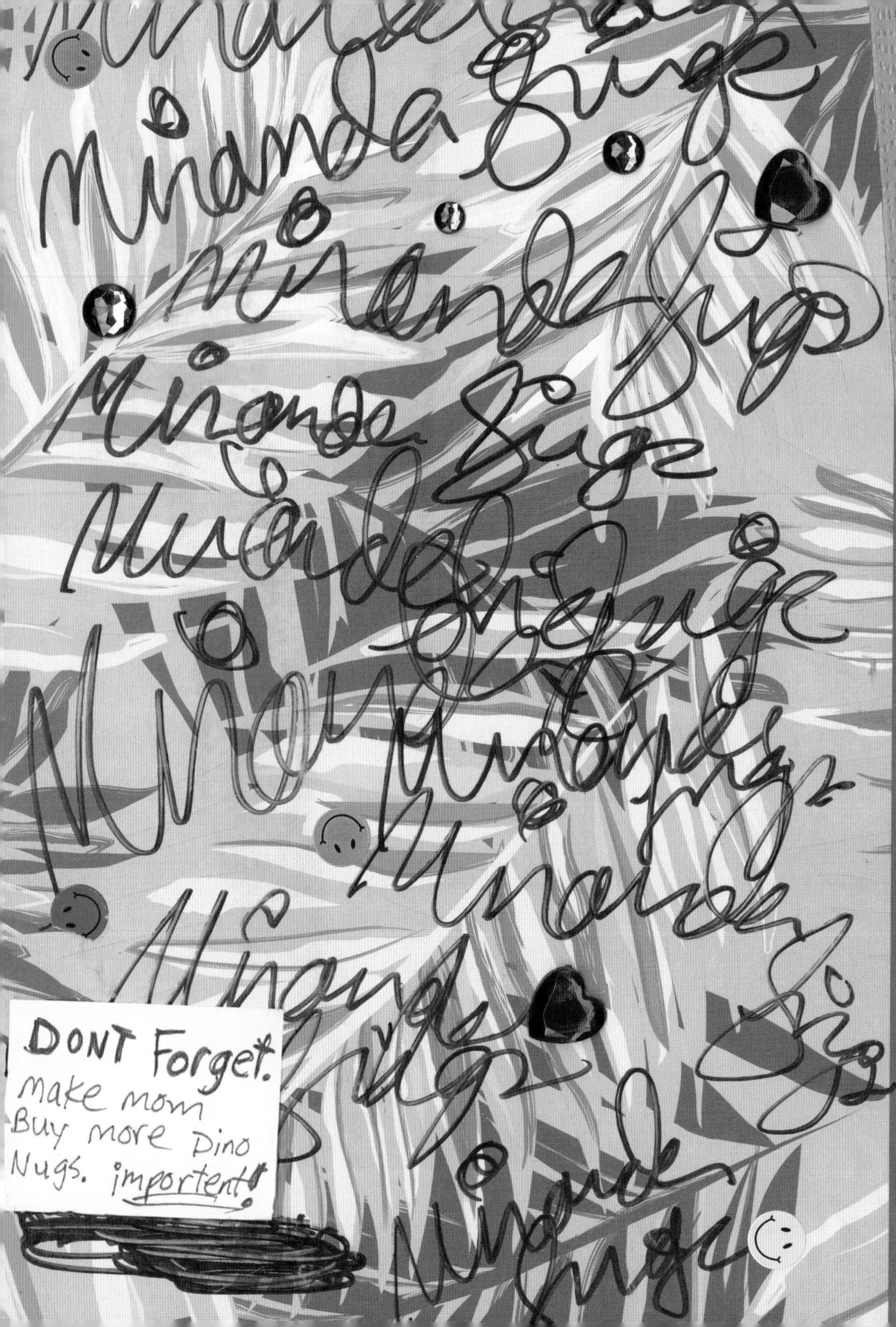
DONT Forget.
make mom
Buy more Dino
Nugs. importent!

Diarrhe #6
EXCELLENT
TOUR!
WELL DONE
YOUTUBE!
WELL DONE
FAMUS!
MASTER
LMNOPRSTUWYABCDEFGHI
Master
Miranda

Miranda Sings
Jan 2, 2018
6:39 PM

Diarrhe #6

is a relly good 1. its during the hole rise of my career so their is lots of adventure and drama. Tour drama, Merch drama, Jerry seinfeld drama, and even chia pet drama. its from like 2010-2015 or somthing. i dont know exacly cuz i dont like math.

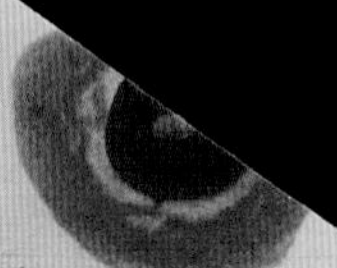

Dear Diarrhe, Miranda Sings 6:49 P.M.

i got the worst hatemail **EVER** today. it said im **NOT** Famus, it said im **ugly**, and it said if i was any more inBred, i would Be a sandwich. **i DONT UNDERstand!** im pretty much the most Famus person in the world By now so i shouldnt Be getting Haters anymore! Even my mom said im Famus so it must Be true. Well, **GUESS WHAT?!** im gonna go on **MORE** tours, im gonna make **LOTS** of viral videos, im gonna sell **TONS** of merch, and im gonna Be more Famus then Beyonsay, Oprah, and the taco Bell dog all combined. **WATCH OUT HATERS! iM TAKiNG OVER THE WORLD & iM GONNA PROOVE YOU ALL WRONG!**

...Butt not today cuz i wanna Finish eating my pasghetti-O's.

♥ Miranda

P.S. Not tomorrow either cuz i might Be tired.

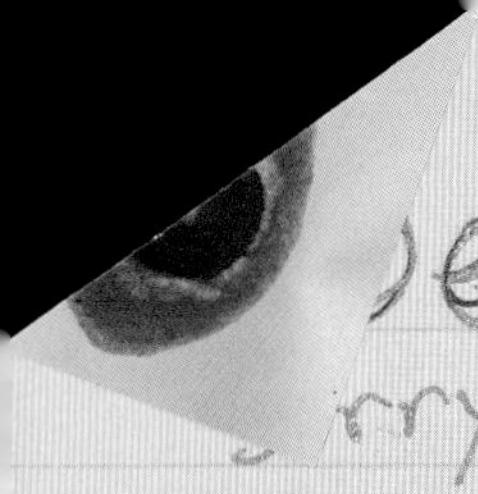

ear Diarrhe,

Miranda Sings
2:49 pm

rry i havnt written in a while Butt im a celebity now so i have a VERY BUSY skedule! Uncle jim says the next thing we need to do for my career is make Brand new, amazing, relly good merch. He said shirts are overrated and dont make good merch cuz not everyone wears shirts. SO... whats the ONE thing that EVERYONE has in common?

The craving to Becum a magichan. Thats rite! im gonna sell magic kits, and im gonna make a FORTUNE! a FOUND a magichan named Chris Ballinger to help make the kits Butt i decided not to pay him cuz Being around me is payment pretty much. its only fair. Also i want all the money for myself.

Anyways, i taped all the tricks From my magic kit to the next page. OK By. ♡ Miranda im so essited to Learn all these magic tricks!!!

I HATE MAGIC!

Dear Diarrhe,

November i dont know i dont care!

Magic is so DUMB! These tricks dont even work at ALL! im so titted off! i could do them FINE when we made the DVD with Chris But now none of the triks are working! This is a total Jip off! I've opend Like 20 magic kits and NONE OF THEM HAVE REAL MAGIC IN THEM! I'm so upset. i have been crying for a whole hour.

actual Tears! im so upset!

And to top it all off, my mom took a sip of MY soda. she said "Oh! it was a acsident!" But Yeh Rite! This is a horibol day. i dont want to talk to you anymore Diarrhe, GOOD NITE!

NOT Love, Miranda

Dear Diarrhe, Miranda Sings 2:111 pm

i Finally did it! i got a Famus BoyFrend! ~~my uncle~~ My Manager has Been trying to get me one For years Becuz it will help me to get more Famuser. Power couples are <u>SO</u> in right now. Soooo.... meet my new BF Joey ~~Graseffa, Grasefin, Grasefica Graserifina~~ Joey G. i met him a long time ago at one of his meet and greets Butt i got kicked out. Then i saw him at a taco Bell event and told him to collaB with me OR ELSE! So he cummed over and we made this video.

IM SO ESSITED! WE ARE GUNNA GET MARRIED! ♡ Miranda

P.S. Patrick is acting relly weird. just cuz <u>HE</u> was my BoyFrend First dosnt mean i cant have MORE Boyfrends. iM FAMUS! Hellooo!!! He clearly doesnt understand science.

Dear Diarrhe,

Miranda Sings
4:1 pm

i have a **BoBBLeHead!** my Magic Kits sold relly well, (like 20 or 21 kits sold so far) so my ~~uncle~~ manager thinks its time to add a new merch item. **BOBBLE HEADS OF ME!** He found a company in China that makes them 4 us. They are relly espensive 2 make, so to save money we are making mom package and ship them all From her Bedroom. Now we wont have to pay someone to do all that. And hear's the Best Part! Guess who was the First Person to Buy one? **LANCE BASS!** i think that mean's im officially part of N'sync!!!

♥ Miranda

mirandaSings midnite

Dear Diarrhe,

im having a **HORRIBOLE DAY!** My uncle RUINED **EVERYTHING!** He Broke my CHIA PET! He ran in to tell me something and nocked it off the shelf... and it spilled everyware and **SHATTERD!** He said it was a accident Butt i <u>KNOW</u> hes Lying. Some of his clothes were on the floor so i kicked them relly hard as punishment. i just uploded a video telling my fans what happened. Here it is →

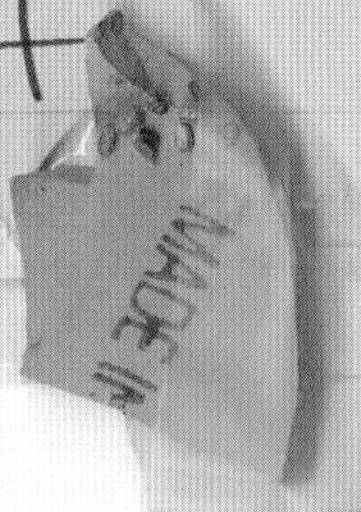

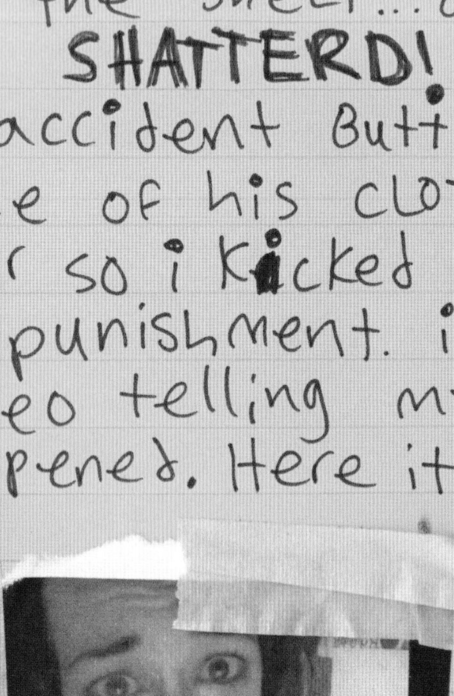

The comments are saying im Being overdramitic Butt im <u>NOT</u>! He ruined my Life and NOW **i HAVE NOTHING TO LIVE FOR!** sinserly, Miranda

P.S. Patrick gave me that chia pet. :(

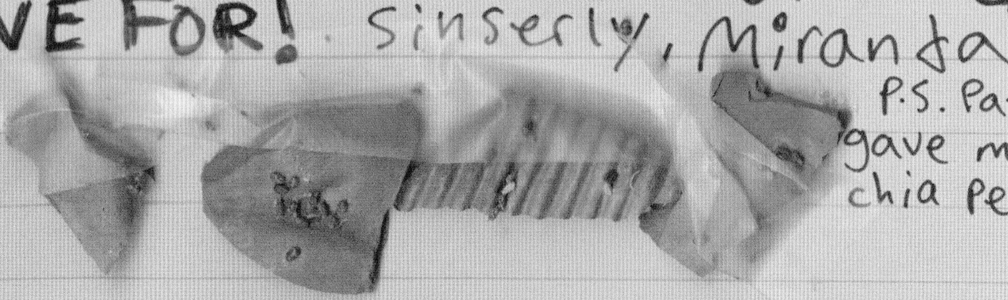

Miranda Sings
4:00 am

Dear Diarrhe,

As you know, Life has Been hard for me recentLy. My chia Pet got ruined, my Mom keeps annoying me, and i Keep getting Hate maiL! Hear is another 1 i got today

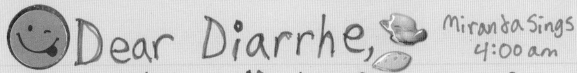

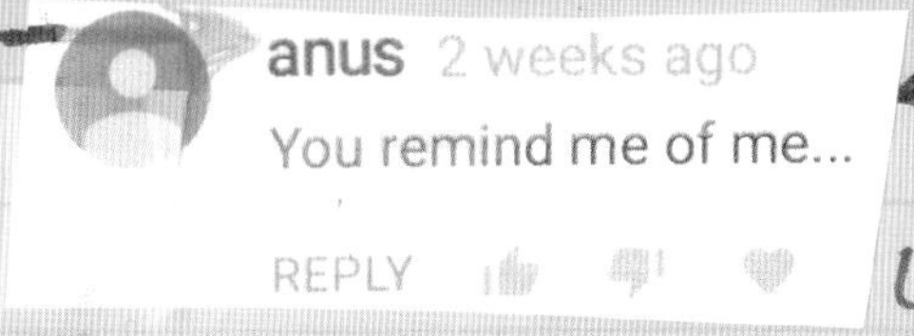
anus 2 weeks ago
You remind me of me...
REPLY

i know that Looks Like a nice comment Butt dont Let it FooL you. its from ANUS! i remind you oF ANUS?! Thats not even the Best part of the Butt! RUDE!

Anyways, aLL this stuFF has Been making me relly sad LateLy. i cry aBout it aLot and some times i FeeL Like i shouLd quit. (Dont you EVER tell ANYONE i said that. its a secret!) Butt i had a show at BirdLand in NYC a coupLe days ago and my Fans Brought me new chia pets cuz they saw my video aBout my Broken one. The haters are mean, my mom is annoying, Butt my Fans make me FeeL Like everything wiLL Be ok.

They teLL me i help them 2 Be confident and happy. They make me wanna Keep going. They understand me when no one else does. So iLL never quit. iLL keep going for them, cuz they deserve it. Butt also cuz i want them to Buy me more stuff.

♡ Miranda

Dear Diarrhe,

Miranda Sings
10:71 pm

i havnt written in a long time cuz i didnt want too. No offense. Butt a lot has happened. i decided i shuld have a TV show about me. im talented, pretty, and the most famus person in the world so a TV show about me wuld be a HIT! So i started going to a lot of different TV places and told them to give me my own show and they said NO. What the heck! i dont no why every1 in this industry looks down on YouTubers. No one respects me! it makes no cents. i work **SO HARD** every single day and still... No respect. its so frustrating! im VERY TITTED OFF!

Love,
Miranda

P.S. i took this photo of myself today after i ate soup.

Dear Diarrhe, Miranda S. i dont no the time.

i got a viral video Today!!!
as you no, i love taking sLurpee Baths. WELL, yesterday i decided to Film my sLurpee Bath To Let my Fans no im a regular girl who takes Baths just Like them! i guess everyone Loved it cuz it got MILLIONS of views! People Love QUALITY CONTENT!
PoLiticks? No thank you.
TaLent? Boring!
Education? GOODBYE!
Taking a sLurpee Bath with my clothes on? Millions of views! i think this is relly gonna help my career. Now iLL deFinitly get the respect i deserve.

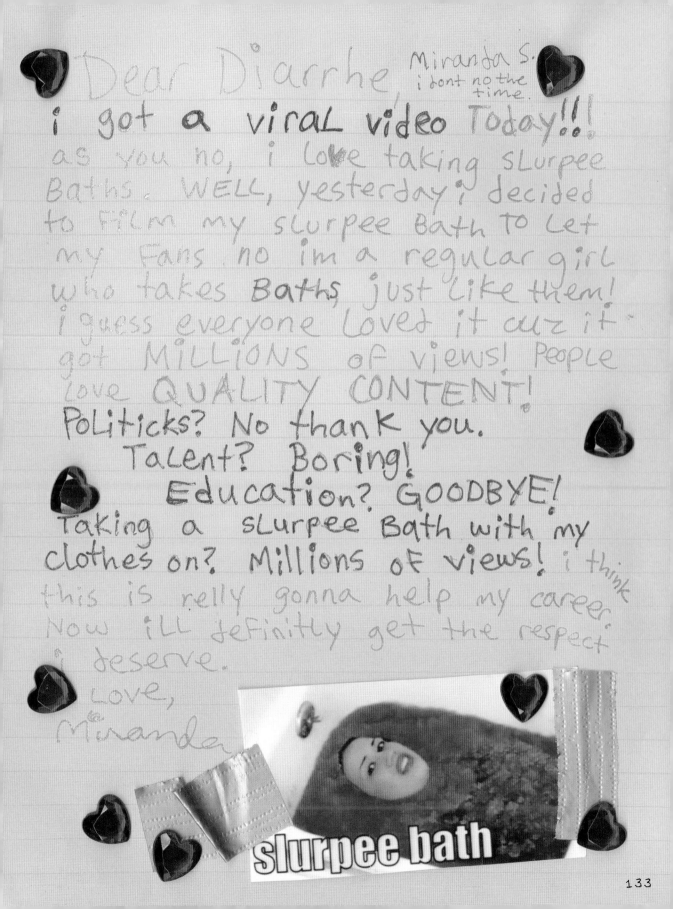

Love,
Miranda

Dear Diarrhe, Miranda Sings 7:04 pm

i decided to start touring alot more Becuz i love traveling and meeting all my Fans.

...Also i love money.

So im gonna start writing in hear aBout my Fon experiences on tour. Hear are some of the places im going in the next couple years—

♡ Miranda

miranda sings
8:02 pm

Dear Diarrhe,

Hi. Since im gonna start touring more i realized im gonna need ALOT of help. i have to hire someone to take care of travel details, get me water, Fan me when im hot etc. So i decided to get a Buttsistant. (i cant say the "A" word cuz its Bad and im not a sinner.) i Found a weird girl on YouTuBe and shes gonna cum on tour with me and Basicaly do everything i say. This is her applicachon

♡miranda

APPLICACHON TO WORK 4 MIRANDA

NAME: Rachel Ballinger

AGE: ~~22~~ no. you LOOK 23

FAVORITE COLOR: ~~Purple~~ Miranda

FAVORITE FOOD: ~~Pizza~~ Miranda

DO YOU LIKE ME: Sure. correct.

AS A FRIEND OR MORE: A Friend good

ARE YOU SUBSCRIBED TO ME?: Yes. good

WILL YOU DO EVERYTHING I SAY?: Sure.

HEADSHOT

your hair is too short. grow it out.

i dont Like this shirt. Dont ware it again.

YOUR Hired.

Dear Diarrhe,

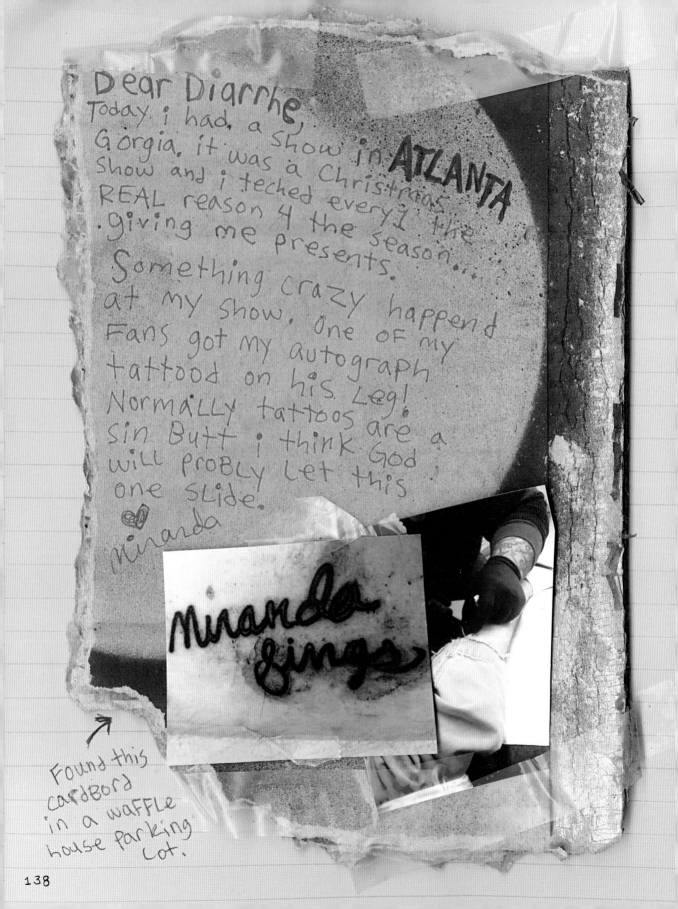

Today i had a show in ATLANTA Gorgia. it was a Christmas show and i teched every1 the REAL reason 4 the season... giving me presents.

Something crazy happend at my show. One of my fans got my autograph tattood on his Leg! Normally tattoos are a sin butt i think God will probly let this one slide.

♡ miranda

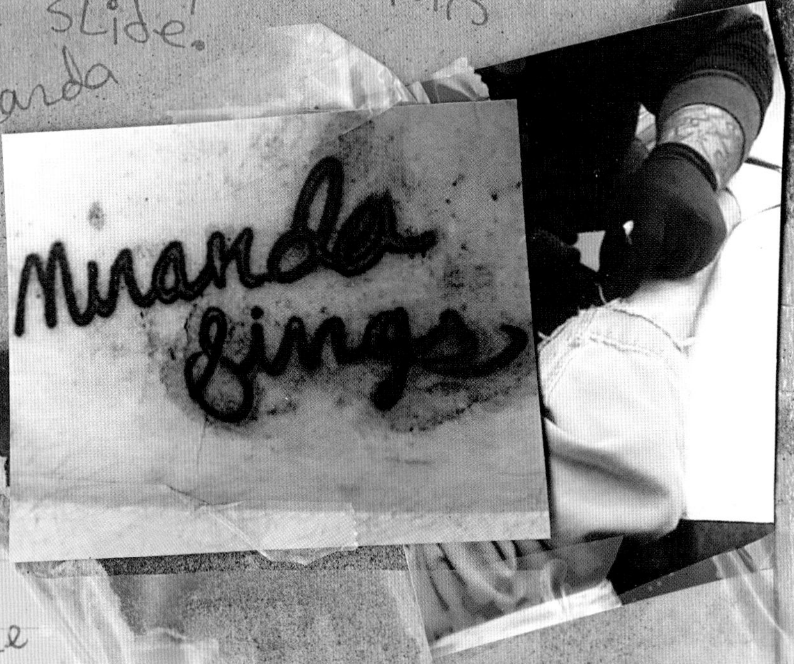

Found this cardBord in a waffle house parking Lot.

Dear Diarrhe,

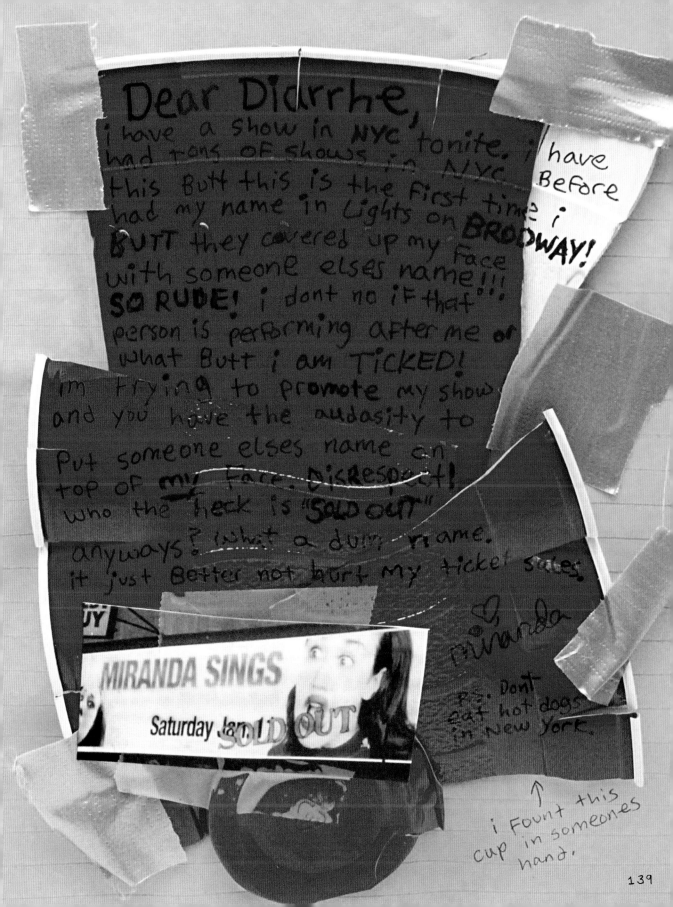

i have a show in NYC tonite. i have had tons of shows in NYC Before this Butt this is the first time i had my name in Lights on BRODWAY! BUTT they covered up my face with someone elses name!!! SO RUDE! i dont no if that person is performing after me or what Butt i am TICKED! im trying to promote my show and you have the audasity to Put someone elses name on top of my face. DISRESPECT! who the heck is "SOLD OUT" anyways? what a dum name. it just Better not hurt my ticket sales.

♡, miranda

P.S. Dont eat hot dogs in New York.

↑ i Fount this cup in someones hand.

Dear Diarrhea

its Been a gr8 couple of days
i got to cum Back to London
Butt this time i came Back
with my Frend and BoyFrend
Frankie Grande.. We got
arrested at Customs cuz
the offiser thot i was
gonna Steal from the
country. just Becuz i said
a joke and said "im gonna
steal all your money and not
pay taxes", doesnt mean its true.
he was so grumpy. Butt they
evenchally Let us go. My
shows sold out every NITE!
it was really FUN.

I got this paper from dinner

and even though
there is a huge
Langugue Barrier in London
the audience still understood
me relly goodly. My fans are
very smart. exsept when they
dont give me presents. Then
they R dum. ♥ Miranda

2 of my
Fans. They
r weird,
Butt they
like me.

me and Frankie
after we got
aressted.

Dear Diarrhe,

i had a show in Detroit tonite and Rachel is SO GRUMPY. i thot we culd drive to all the shows this week cuz they are all in america. i got off stage, we got in the rental car, and i told Rachel to start driving. She said, "WHAT?! Thats 11 hours! Why are we driving and not FLYing?! Now i have to Drive thru the night and do a show tomorrow with NO SLEEP?" umm... get over it. She's such a BaBy.

How was i supossed to no the drive wuld Be that Far? anyways, im gonna go to sleep in the car now. We have a Big day 2morrow and i need my rest.

♥ miranda

i found this Bag from a Lady with groseries.

Dear Diarrhe,

i performed in DuBuque, iowa today. The show was in a Movie theater. i performed iN Front of the Screen where you watch Movies, and they didnt have spotLights so they just left all the Lights on in the hole theater. at First i was relly excited to Be in a movie theater cuz i thot i would get Lots of free popcorn. Butt i didnt. **AND** my dressing room was a Projector room with nothing in it except a mattress with a Bunch of pee stains on it.

and ONLY **ONE** of those stains was From me.

#TOURLiFE

♡ Miranda

↑ i Found this Box under the pee mattress

Dear Diarrhe,

we had a Emergency Landing in Vegas yesterday on our way to ScotLand Becuz of tecknical difficulties. They said it was cuz a passenger's T.V. wasnt working Butt i think it had to do with the Fact that one of the wings was smoking. ANYWAYS, while we were waiting For our plane to get Fixed, i Found a nice spot on the ground By a trash can to eat my stale airport sandwitch. An angry Lady in a Beanie came up to me and told me i was destroying my tookie By sitting on the cement. She said there are chemicals in the cement that go up inside of girls and ruin there insides. She yelled at me for 15 Minutes about it. Now, im NO scientist, Butt that sounds Like a resipee to make a Robot. i thanked her For the tip and sat there For 4 more hours hoping for the Best.

Love,

Miranda

P.S. i didnt turn into a robot

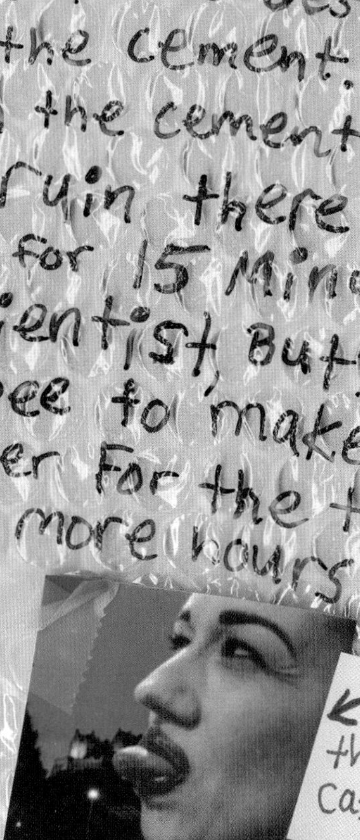

← me Licking the EdinBurgh castle today.

Miranda Sings
6:02 pm

Dear Diarrhe,

ive Been Touring **on** and **OFF** aLOT in the last Few years and i Love it Butt im glad i'm home for a Little Bit. i decided to spend some time at home in tacoma to Focus on getting More Famuser and work on Becumming president. ALSO i relly missed Patrick. i have **LOTS** of Boyfrends By now Butt he is my Favorite i think. (Dont tell him i said that.) He's the onLy one who makes me Feel Like i have gas when im with him. its proBLy cuz he gives me Froze toes posickLes and they have aLot of dairy in them.

i took this picture for him 2day... →

i hope he Likes it.

Gotta go.. im Bored of writing and my eye is ichy.

♡ miranda

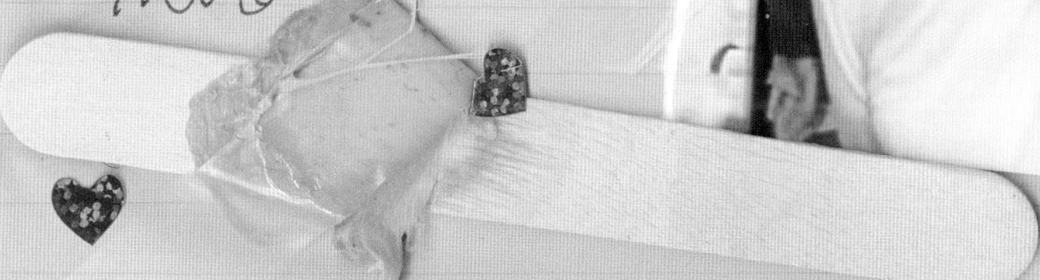

Dear Diarrhe, Mirandasings
Nighttime

its Monday. That means i have 2 upload a video on my YouTuBe channel. UGH! why did i ever say i wuld do **2** videos a week? This is so much work and i am WAY TOO STRESSED to make a video today. My mom woke me up at 10:30 am when i was having a <u>relly</u> good dream. SO DISrespectFULL! **THEN** there wasnt any "oops all Berries" Left so i had to eat plane "capten crunch". And After THAT i got a ich on the Bottom of my Foot AFTER i put on my shoes. i wiggled my Foot relly hard inside the shoe to try to get the ich Butt it didnt satisfy me at all SO as you can see, im WAY too stressed to make a video... Butt I HAVE

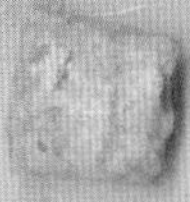

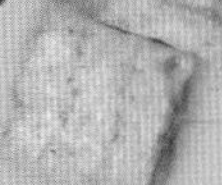

too do it For my fans. im a slave to my work. How will my Fans survive if i dont uplod a video??? They wont Be aBLe to Function. ugh... im just gonna go Film something relly Fast and get it over with. BrB.

- - - - - - - - - - - - -

ok, so i just quikLy wrote a song and posted it. i did it in Like 10 minutes and didnt relly care aBout it. HopeFully Not too many people will see it. its called "Where my Baes at"

Gotta go... mom made Dino chicken nuggets.

♡ miranda

P.S. my Foot still iches.

my video

Dear Diarrhe,

Miranda Sings
12:39pm

Today somthing weird happend. A guy named jerry called me and asked me to get coffee with him. i never heard of him Before Butt someone told me he was a "comedien" so i thought i would try to help him get Famus cuz i Love charity work. We drove around in his weird Little car for a while, got some coffee and he ate some gross diner food. i tried relly hard to help him with his career Butt i think he just doesnt have what it takes. Bless him for trying tho. Anyways, im starving so i gotta go.

Bye.

♡Miranda

P.S. i forgot what i was gonna say. Nevermind.

Dear Diarrhe,

my sister Left this note on my Bed today. SO many things wrong with this! She went in to my room witch is OFF LIMITS!

Miranda-
I am so proud of you.
Love you.

~Emily

She put something on my Bed and what if i didnt see it? i Could have choked on it in my sleep and DIED! or worse- i could have gotten a paper cut! she's So rude!

its relly weird how my Fans dont know about her... Butt she doesnt want anyone to know we are sisters cuz she's "embarrased" of me.

This is hard for me 2 admit Butt... she's right.

Being related to me IS embarrassing. :(

it must Be SO embarassing for her to Be relaxed to someone who is way more talented, Pretty and perfect then her. poor girL...

i gotta admit- Life has Been crazy with all this Fame and its Been relly nice to know i have a sister around to annoy any time i want.

i relly dont Like her... Butt i DO Love her. (Dont tell her i said that)

♡ Miranda

Dear Diarrhe,

Miranda Sings
2:41 am

i was on the jimmy Fallon show tonite. That old guy Jerry Seinfeld called me the other day and asked me if i wanted to be on the jimmy Fallon show with him. i think maybe the only way he wuld be able to get on a big show like that is if he had a big celebrity with him. So naturaly he asked me. i played pictionary with jimmy Fallon, Martin short, and Jerry. on LIVE TV! i won the game i think. it was my First time on a talk show butt i was the prettiest one their so they will probly ask me to be the new host soon. jimmys cute and all... butt im better. No offense,

♡ Miranda

Miranda Sings
7:11 pm

Dear Diarrhe,

its Been a while since i Last wrote 2 you, Butt i have **Big News...**

NetFLix and HBO called. They Both want to do my T.V. show!

i dont no what to do. im SO stressed. i have such a huge desicion to make. This could change my entire Life forever. should i have Mexican or italian food for dinner? ugh... i cant decide.

Anyways, im gonna do the NetFLix Original series.

♡ miranda

Diarrhe #7

Fan male

Fan art

Miranda's Mirfandas!

Fan comments

Fan presents

Miranda Sings
Jan 2, 2018
7:12 PM

This is my Fan Diarrhe.
im relly Famus Now
so i have LOTS oF Fans
and they are always
giving me Letters,
art, presents, and a
Bag oF raw Bacon once.
i put a BuNCh oF Fan
StuFF in this Diarrhe
to always remember
how Famus i am.

Dear Diarrhe,
i just got this Brand new jurnal and i decided to deadicate it 2 my Mirfandas. in Case you dont no what that is- hear is the definichon.

Mirfanda
(mer-fan-duh)
noun, verb, adjective, smart people and more

Definichon:
A person who is obsessed with the incredibel superstar Miranda Sings. They love Miranda more then anything in the world and they usually dress just like Miranda and copy her because they Are relly smart. d. Anyone who is not a Mirfanda is a HATER and cannot be trusted.

MirFanda

its importent 2 no the diference Between a **FAN** and a **HATER**. You can tell By Looking at clues in the comments.

MirFandas

They say nice things Like "OMG" (Oh, Miranda's great)

Ricky Dillon 3 years ago
omg
REPLY 722

They give you relly nice compliments.

Shanhanhania 6 months ago
she looks like the type of girl who would microwave her pet hamster
REPLY

They say they Love you in every Language.

Adeleivalivas 2 months ago
eres estúpido

They are vulnerabol and confide in you. i RESPONDED to Rylisom and told her to get a pad right away.

Rylisom 3 days ago
When I here'd you sing my eras bled
REPLY

HATERS!

Kira 2 weeks ago
Miranda your stupid.
REPLY

They say Bad words.

They talk about gross things Like old people.

Wisemananan 2 weeks ago
I showed this to my grandma and she died laughing
REPLY

they Lie

Zoeeneeenee 9 hours ago
I hate u
REPLY

Jeanuijk 6 months ago
Y DO PEPOL WACH THIS STOOPID DUM BINCH
REPLY

They dont speak English good.

They dare you to do very offensive things.

XxBolBolaxX 2 months ago
I dare you to dab in one of your vids
REPLY 2

Fan Gifts

My MirFandas Love to give me Presents. Hear are some of My Favorites . . .

Lots of dolls of me

a nun

A sign 4 my Door

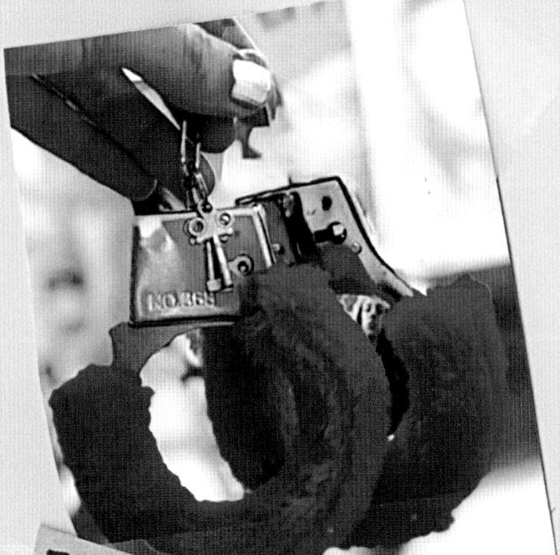

Fun handcuffs

ugly shirt from Jerry Seinfeild

Bag of hair

Drama Masks
paper Mashay head with my real eyes inside
Lots of hair Clips
HATERS BACK OFF
Lots of hand made Clothes
MIRANDA
Lots of Braslets
a Little cake roll thats only a Little smushed
A huge puppet of myself.
Tiny crocks in case I ever shrink
a cat collar of someones dead pet cat

Fan Letters

i get tons of Letters from my Fans every single day. They tell me how much they Love me, they ask me 4 advice, tell me i save their Lives and ask me to Follow them on twitter. Here are some examples...

DEAR MIRANDA,
I AM YOUR #1 FAN! YOU ARE THE MOST TALENTED, BEAUTIFUL, PERFECT, AMAZING, INCREDIBEL, INSPIRING PERSON IN THE WHOLE WORLD AND I WILL NEVER STOP SUPPORTING YOU! LOVE YOU!

LOVE,
YOUR #1 FAN
UNCLE JIM

see? i save peoples lifes.

you shuld becum a orphan.

i Lost this.

Dear Miranda,

Oh My gosh I cant believe I'm writing you a letter right now and you're actually reading it! You are my Hero. I am 14 years old and you literally saved my life I'm dead ~~se~~ serious you literally saved my life cuz like one day I was like really sad and stuff and then I watched one of your videos and then I was like not sad and like you literally saved my life I'm not even kidding. My parents hate you and all my friends think you're lame so I'm not going to watch you're videos anymore. But I ... write and say ...ou saved my ...f see why my ...ed. You're kind ... and your lipstick ...zy and I dont ...amous, but I'm ... you! Have a ...

...ssa

Follow me on twitter!

Bad word!

...s how my aunt died. It w... honestly one of the worst days o... my life, but your videos made me smile when nothing else could. Thats why I want you to have my aunt's diomand necklace tha... was passed down to me. Please take really good care of the necklace. It means a lot to me. Also, since I gave you a real diamond can you please follow me on twitter? and insta? and snapchat? If you dont, send me the necklace back. I don't want you to have it. Love you.

~Rachel

no.

Oh my gosh that must have Been so scary. i was locked in the closet once for 2 hours and i was STARVING. proud of myself for inspiring you to get out of the closet.

Hi Miranda,
I just wanted to say thank you. Your confidence inspired me to come out of the closet. I finally feel free and happy. Living in fear and darkness for 15 years is finally over and I have you to thank for it. I ... Journe... wi... the ... of me ... cult ... first ... hat ... as

Thank you!

Dear Miranda,

I am a stay at home mother of 3 young girls and I must say, I am extremely disappointed in the example you are setting for my children. I know you're very famous but that doesn't mean you can get away with this terrible behavior. My kids love your youtube show and watch it all day long while I'm busy. Yesterday I heard them watching a video where you were eating an unbelievable amount of candy. How dare you! My children are not allowed to have sugar and you put me in a very uncomfortable position where I had to explain to my 3, 5, and 7 year old that some people make the disgusting decision to put that poison into their bodies. THEN I heard you loudly singing a pop song. I do NOT let my children listen to pop music, but now they want to listen to it because of you. To top it all off, this morning I heard my 7 year old say "If someone like Miranda can be confident and become famous, I can do anything!". This is a horrible mindset to promote to children because it sets them up for failure. What if they want to be a youtube person or a pop star some day? That is an unrealistic goal and they will most likely end up with depression because of the false sense of hope YOU instilled in them. If my children grow up to be drug addicts, or in prison, I will be sending YOU the bill. You need to THINK about what you put on the internet for your millions of viewers. You are responsible for the lives of every single person watching you. GROW UP. If you had a yelp account I would give you ONE STAR!

Sincerely,
A very frustrated mother

These kids sound relly smart. if this mom keeps Being a Butt ill take the kids. (Not relly i dont like kids. No offense)

Fan Art

i get thousands of Fan art drawings of myself every year. Obviusly alot of my Fan art is on the wall in my room. Butt unfortunatly some of my Fans arent very talented and they're drawings arent worthy of Being on my Famus wall. iLL show you what i mean...

ALice • Age 2 • Dublin, irland

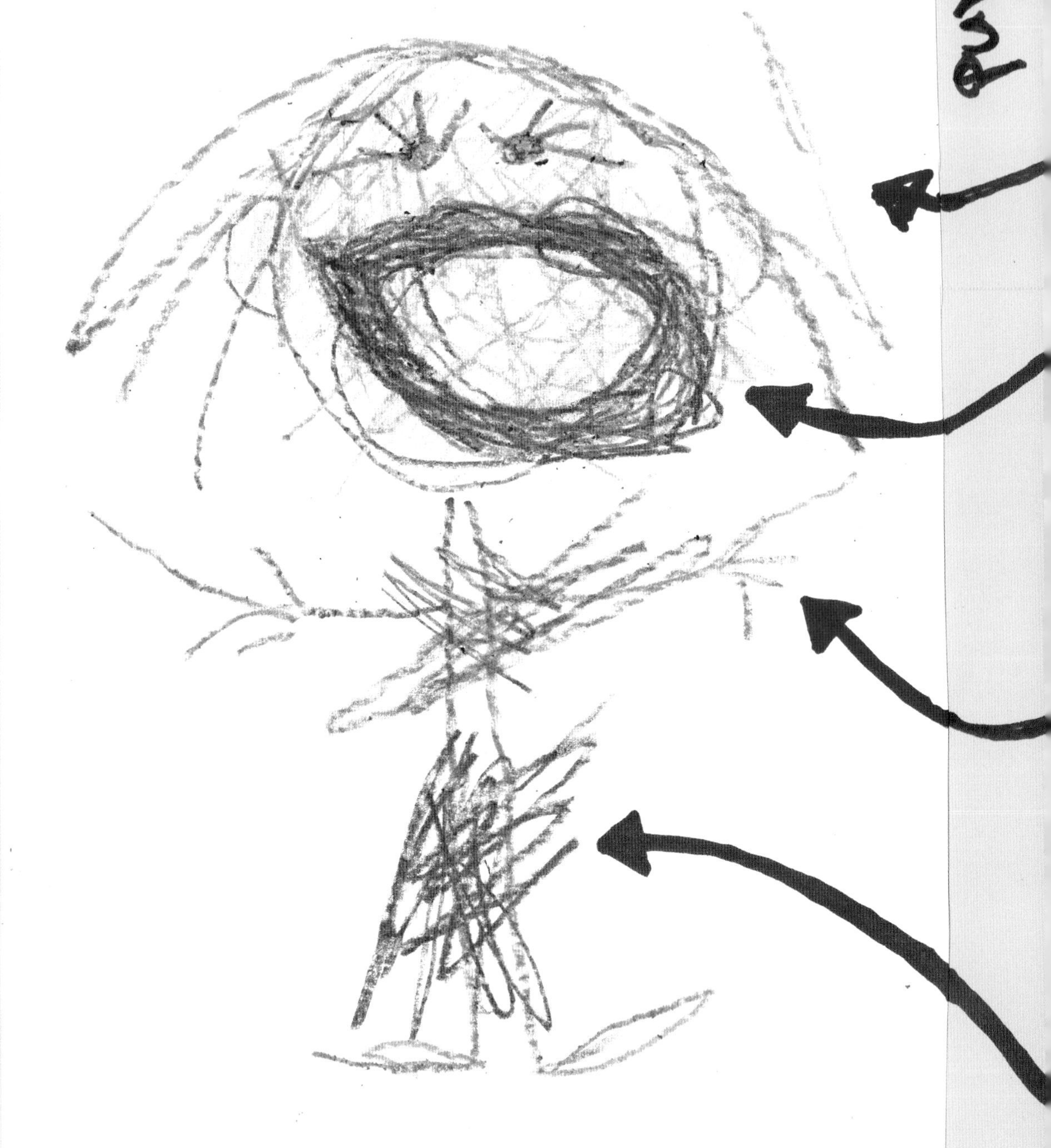

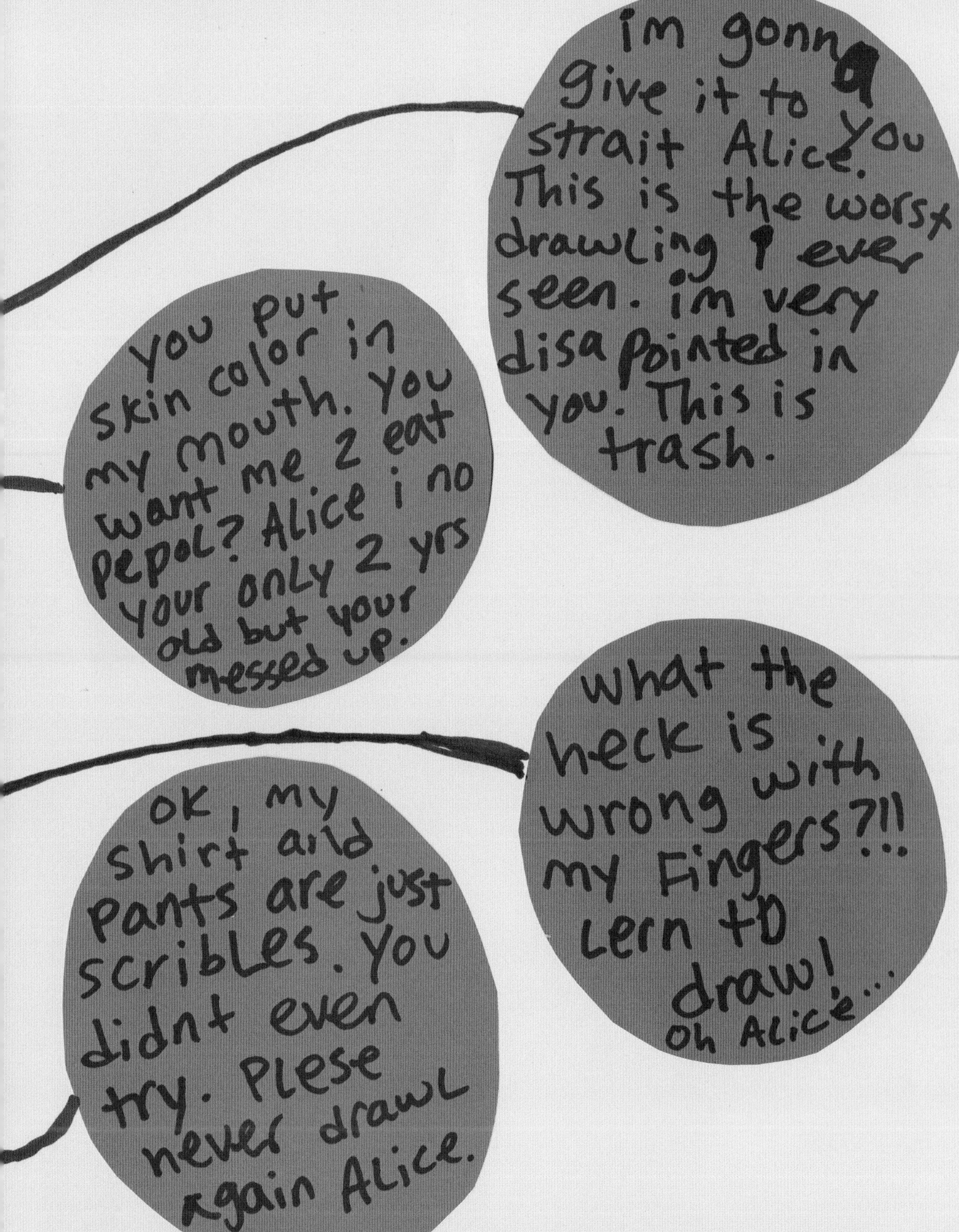
im gonna give it to you strait Alice. This is the worst drawling i ever seen. im very disapointed in you. This is trash.
You put skin color in my mouth. You want me 2 eat pepol? Alice i no your only 2 yrs old but your messed up.
what the heck is wrong with my Fingers?!.. Lern tO draw! Oh Alice...
OK, my shirt and pants are just scribles. You didnt even try. Plese never drawl again Alice.

Jake • Age 8 • L.A., CA

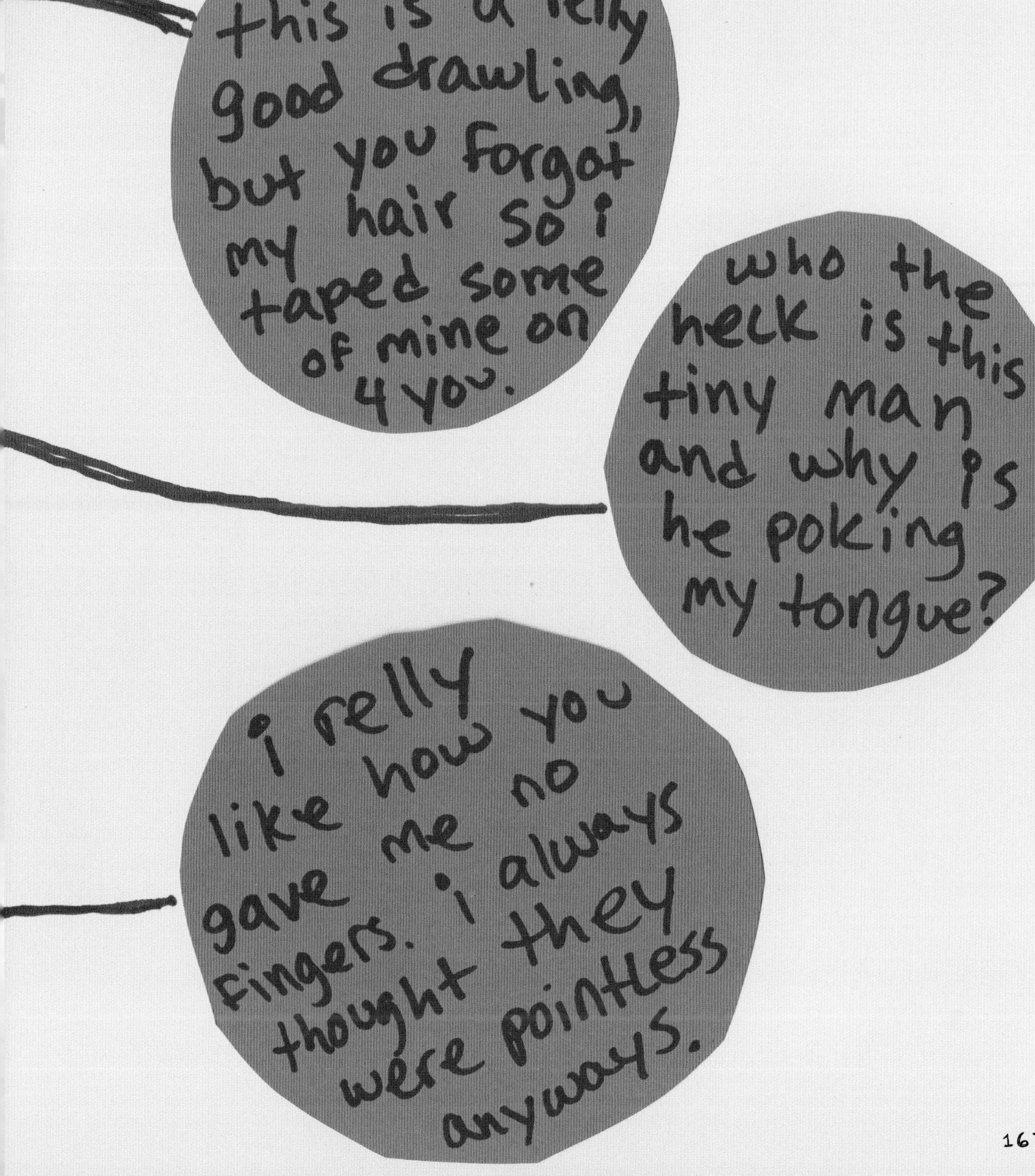
Jake, this is a relly good drawling, but you forgot my hair so i taped some of mine on 4 you.
who the heck is this tiny man and why is he poking my tongue?
i relly like how you gave me no fingers. i always thought they were pointless anyways.

Rachel • 26 • Galt, CA

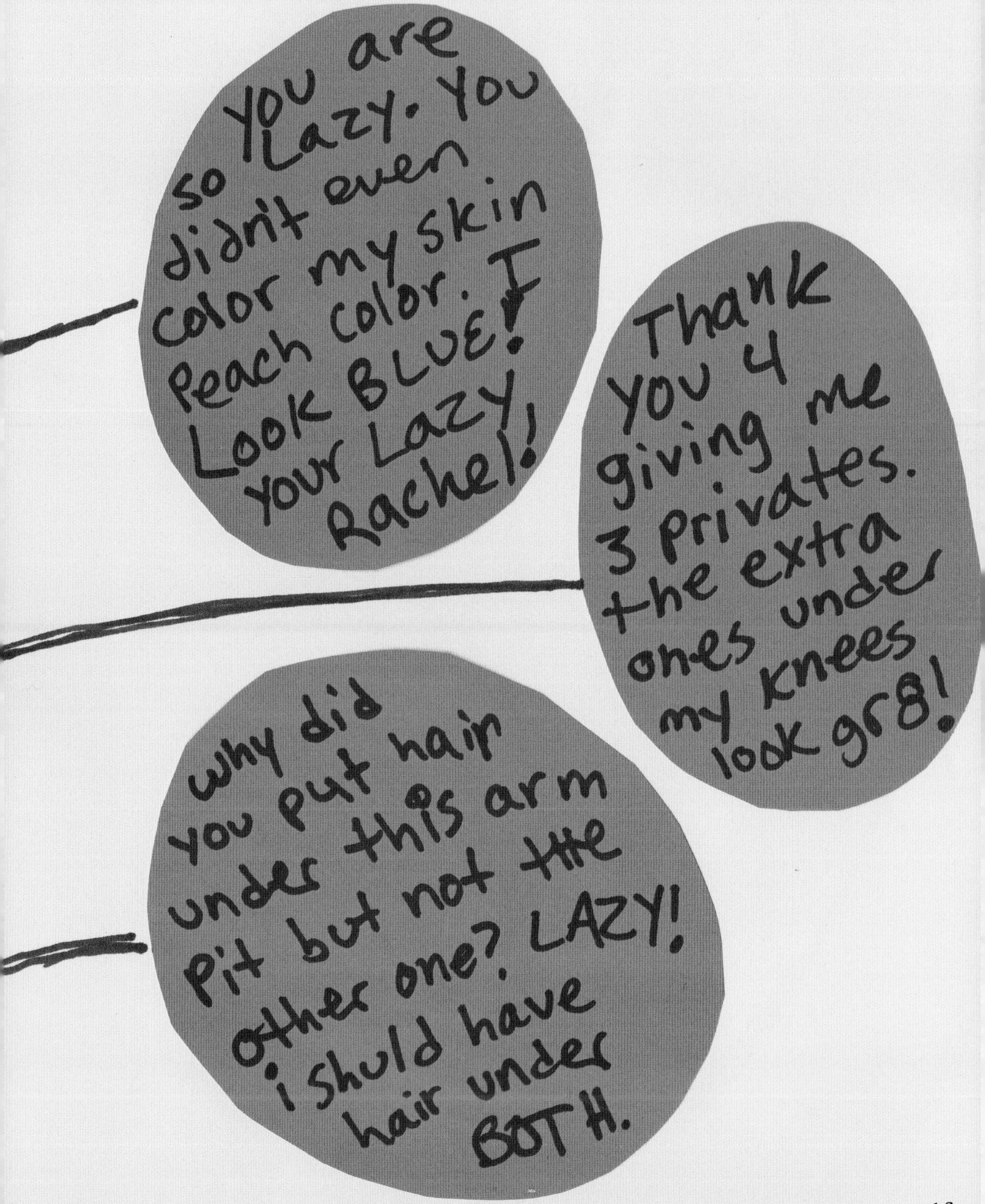
You are so Lazy. You didn't even color my skin Peach color. I Look BLUE! your Lazy, Rachel!
Thank you 4 giving me 3 Privates. the extra ones under my knees look gr8!
why did you put hair under this arm pit but not the other one? LAZY! i shuld have hair under BOTH.

Parker • Age 4 • Santa Barbra, CA

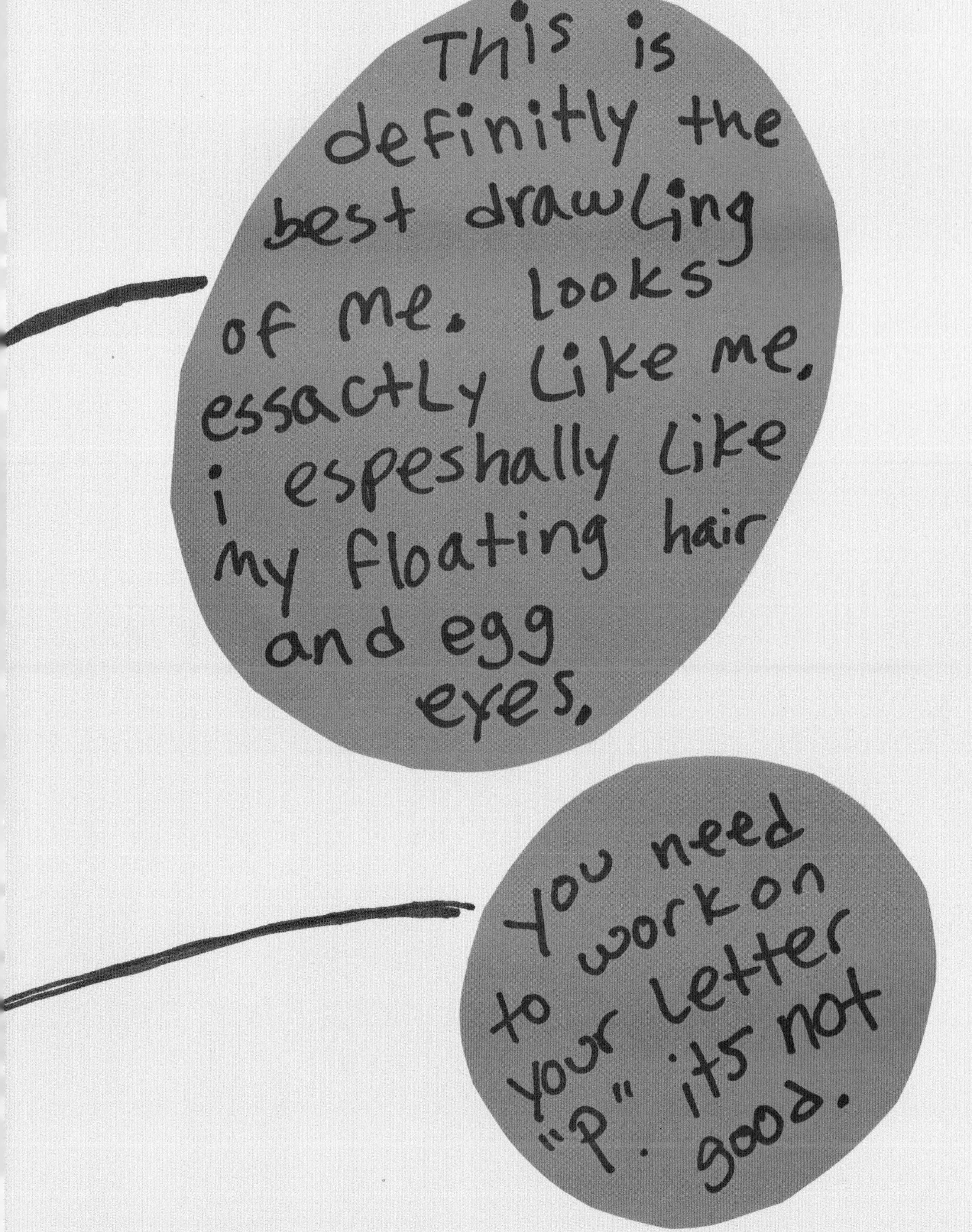
This is definitly the best drawling of me. looks essactLy Like me. i espeshally Like my floating hair and egg eyes.
You need to work on your Letter "p". its not good.

Kory • Age 25 • Upland, CA

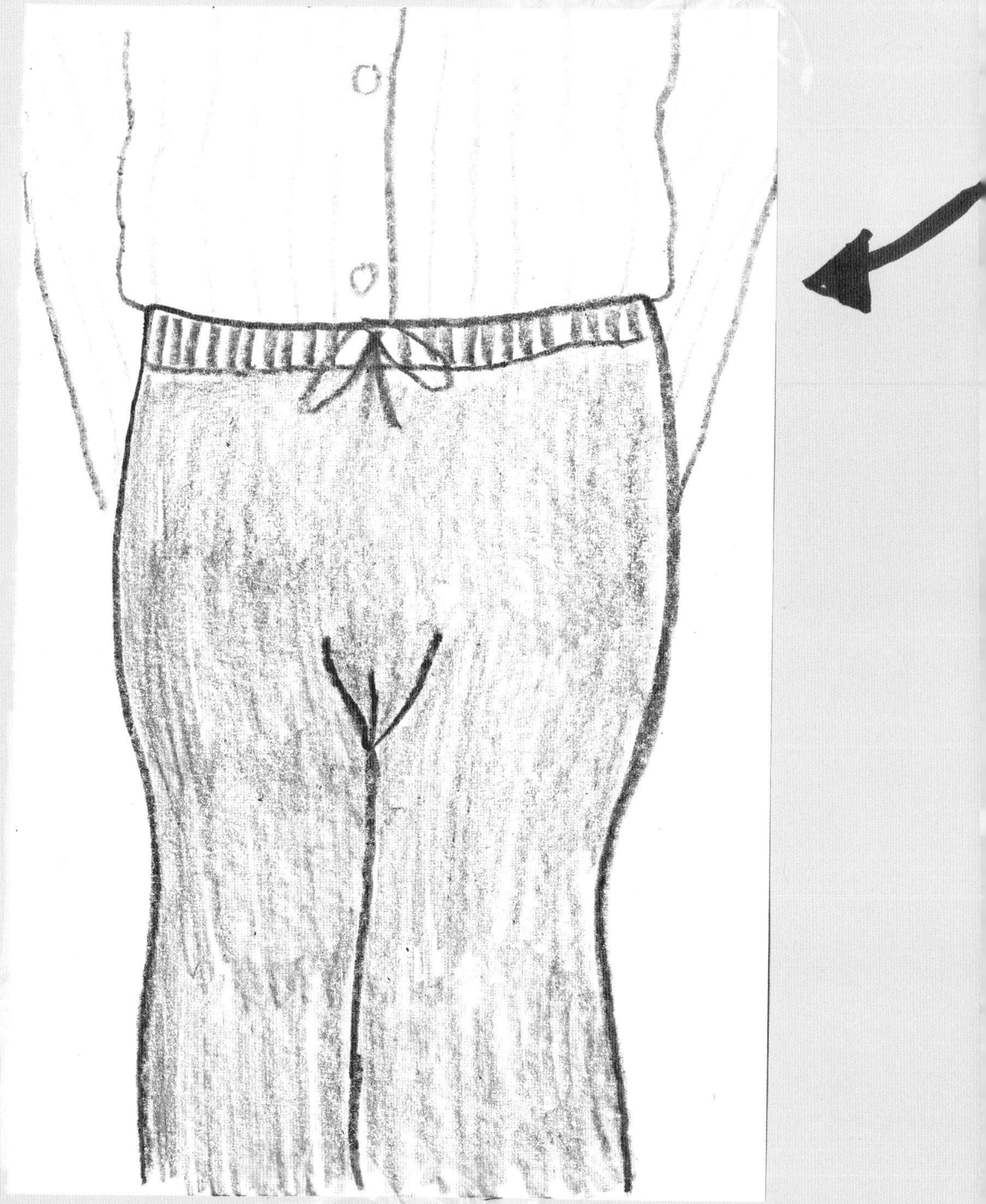

This drawling
is relly good but
you 4got to drawl
my head and toes.
i drew them 4 you.
cut them out & tape
them on the drawling.
Take a PIC and TWeet
it to me!
@MirandaSings
#IFixedTheArt.

MOLLY • Age 6 • Goleta, CA

what is this gang sign? you are only 6 and you know about gang signs? ill pray 4 you.
is this a Front or a butt or a worm?
why is this foot so big and where are my toes? Did somone step on my foot? why is it swolen? also im missing fingers too. This is a ripoff.
F-
im not sure if this is a ice cream or a microphone... but why is it peeing?

Angela • Age 11 • New Mexico

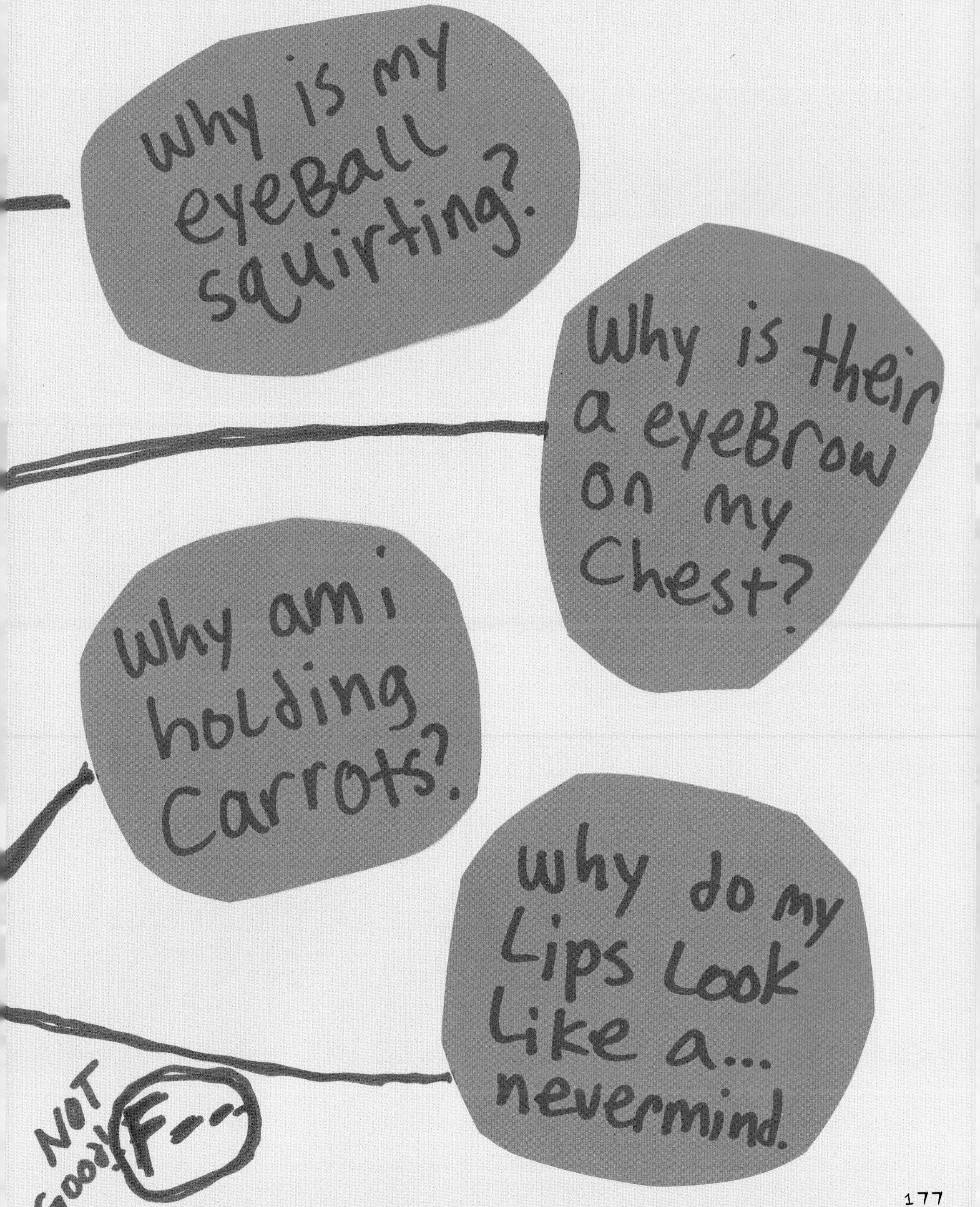

Why is my eyeBall squirting?
Why is their a eyeBrow on my Chest?
Why am i holding Carrots?
Why do my Lips Look Like a... nevermind.
NOT GOOD!
F---

Tyler • Age 14 • Portlend, OR

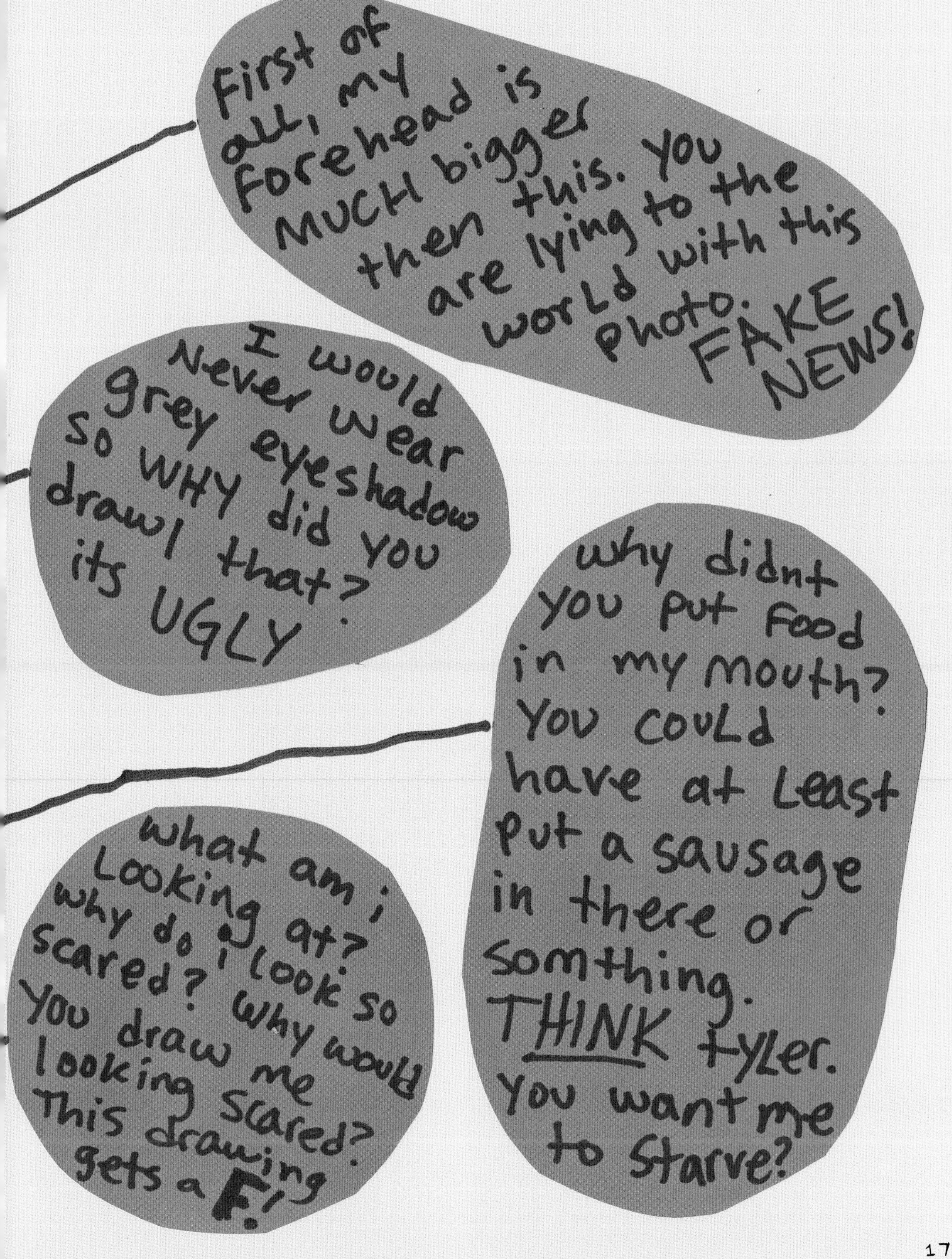
First of all, my forehead is MUCH bigger then this. You are lying to the world with this photo. FAKE NEWS!
I would Never wear grey eyeshadow so WHY did you drawl that? its UGLY
why didnt you put food in my mouth? You could have at Least put a sausage in there or somthing. THINK tyler. You want me to starve?
what am i Looking at? why do i look so scared? why would you draw me looking scared? This drawing gets a F!

Heather • Age 15 • Azusa, CA

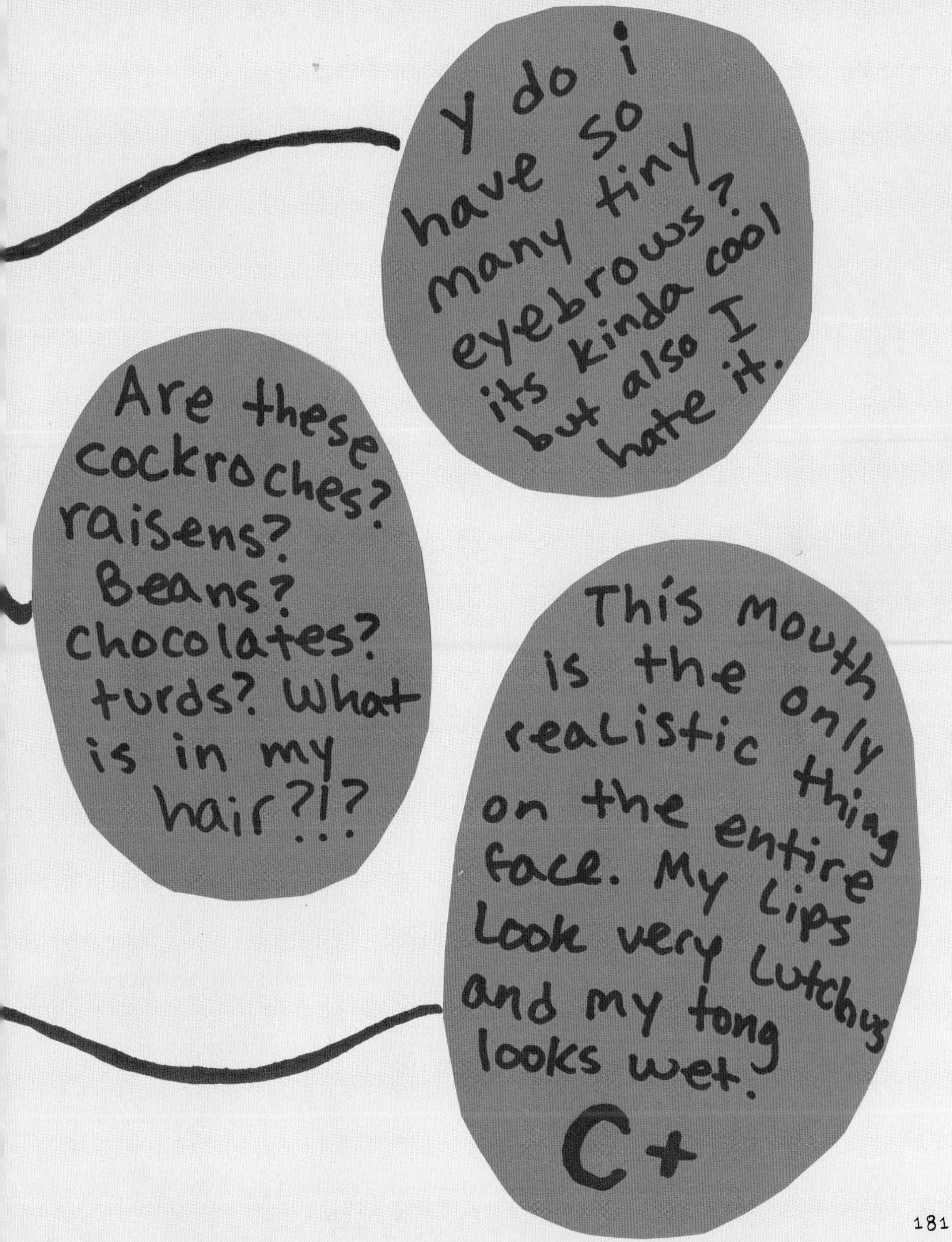
Y do i have so many tiny eyebrows? its kinda cool but also I hate it.
Are these cockroches? raisens? Beans? chocolates? turds? What is in my hair?!?
This mouth is the only realistic thing on the entire face. My Lips Look very Lutchys and my tong looks wet.
C+

Daisy • Age 12 • Sydney, Austraylia

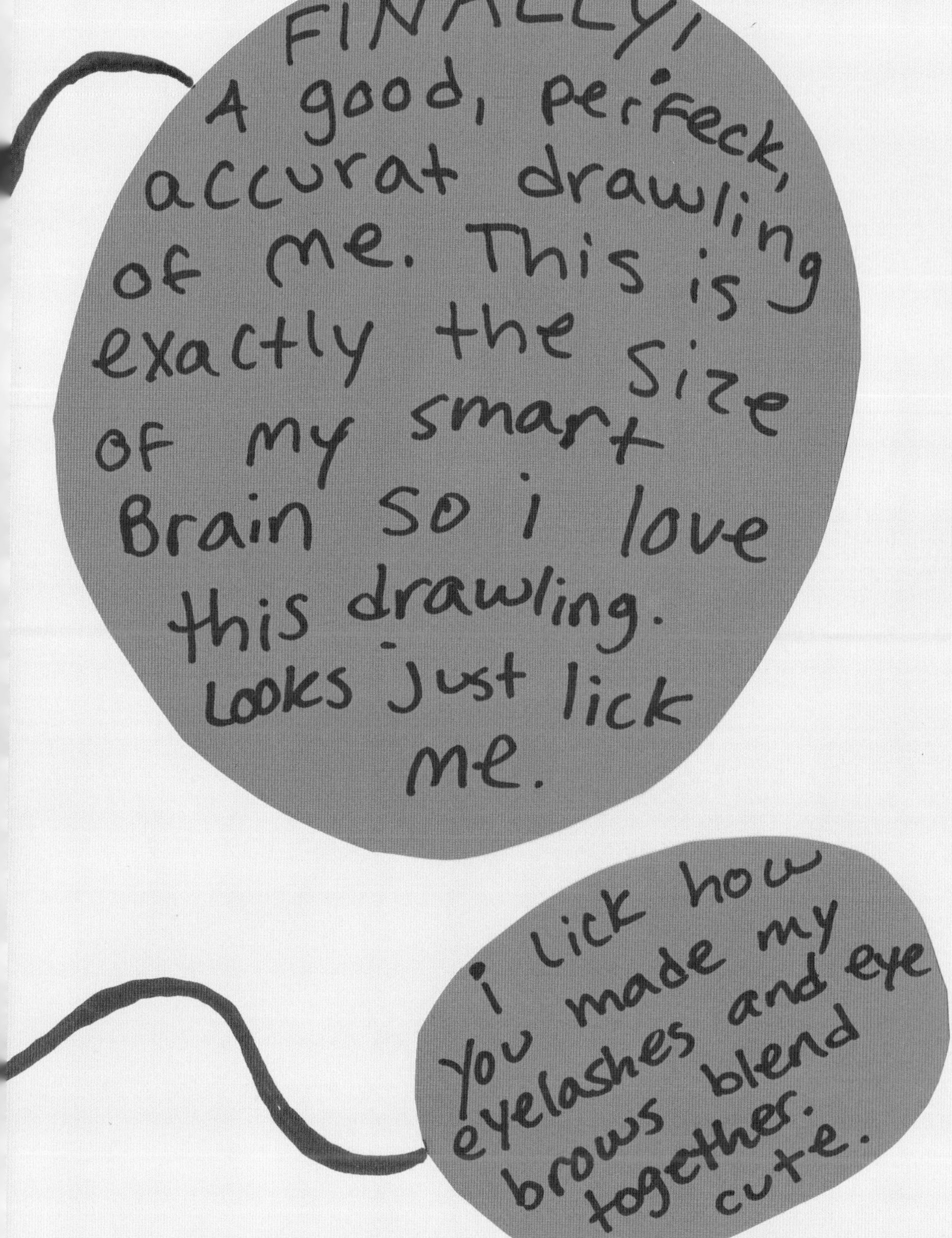
FINALLY! A good, perfeck, accurat drawling of me. This is exactly the size of my smart Brain so i love this drawling. Looks just lick me.
i lick how you made my eyelashes and eye brows blend together. cute.

Eric • Age ? • New Jersey

Not gonna lie. This is a incredibel drawing of me. one of the best i ever seen. Thank you Eric for actualy haveen talent.

love the extra eyelashes you put on my cheeks. i always wanted eyelashes their.

This is Probly the best part. A wifi signal on my chin? Dreams cum true kids!

only 4 Strands of hair wich means it wont take long to do my hair. A+++

so as you can See Diarrhe, some of my Fans have no Talent, some of my Fans have a little talent, and some of my Fans have Lice... cuz i have it rite now and i hugged a lot of them at a show resently.

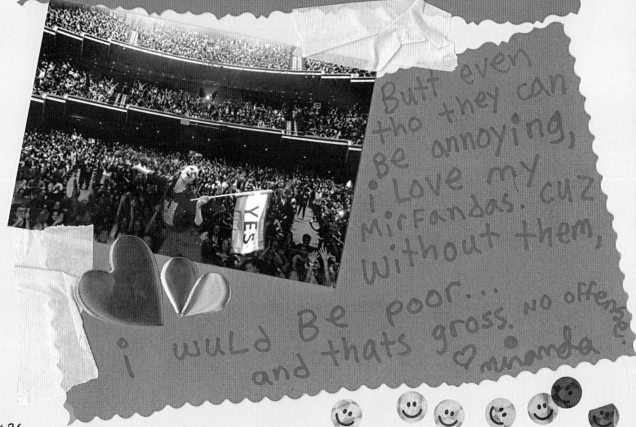

Butt even tho they can Be annoying, i Love my MirFandas. cuz without them, i wuld Be poor... and thats gross. no offense.

♡ miranda

MirFandas=BFF

i gave them Lice.
She made me itch.
i culd smell her meno-Pause.
She made me want 2 end the meet and greet.
he seems moldy.
i dont remember meeting her...
She had wet Skin
her Breth smelled Like old Bandaids.
She reminded me of a scaB.
This photo gave me diaree-uh.
meeting him Made me wanna eat hot dogs.
She smelled Like hamsters

#1 FAN
AWESOME!
Miranda
I'm your
Biggest
FAN!

Diarhe#8
Master
ABCDEFGHILMNOPRSTUWY
Master

Miranda Sings
Jan 2, 2018
8:02 PM

Diarrhe #8 is

my current diarrhe, my First Bus Tour, Behind the scenes of my NetFLix Show and my PLans 4 the Future are aLL in this Journal. its not Finished yet cuz im stiLL writing in it every Day Butt its reLLy good, no offense.

Dear Diarrhe,

Miranda Sings
Aug 4, 2015
11:20 pm oclock.

i got a Brand new Diarrhe! So much has happened. i wrote a Book! its called "Selp-Helf"! its a Book on how to Be a human.

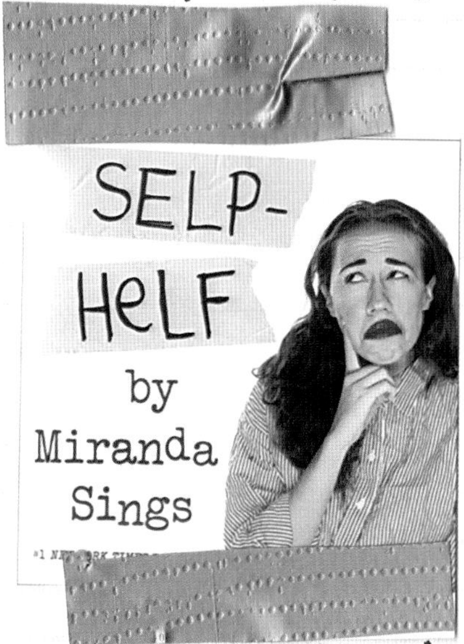

i just Finished my Book tour at the mall of America and my Book publishers just called. They told me im a New York Times Best selling auther. i told them to change it to "Tacoma, Washington Times Best selling auther" Becuz im not from NYC Butt they Are dum and wont change it. idiots...

Love,
miranda

P.S. i dont no if you remember, Butt Netflix is giving me my own show. We R shooting it next year. it Better Be good or im sueing.

Mood: good and hungry

Dear Diarrhe,

Miranda Sings
Aug 5, 2015
3:02 pm

Guess what! i'm doing a **BUS TOUR!** ive Been touring for years Butt i have never done a Big Fancy tour Like this Before! i Feel Like Aaron Carter! One proBLem tho. They said there is no pooping on the Bus. Butt this tour is almost a month Long. These people must have alien Butts cuz no one can clench that hard for that Long. i have allready pooped twice and we havent even Left the parking Lot yet.

Anyways, i never got to do Summer Camps when i was Little so i decided to do my OWN summer camp with my Fans for this tour. **Miranda CAMP!**

♡ Miranda

mood: excited and constipated

i decided to have maching Frendship Braslets with all my Fans. We are selling these at all the shows.

This is a PP patch my Fans can earn if they partisipate... or if they Buy it.

These are the tour Shirts. They have all my tour dates on the Back cuz i Love gettin dat Promo!

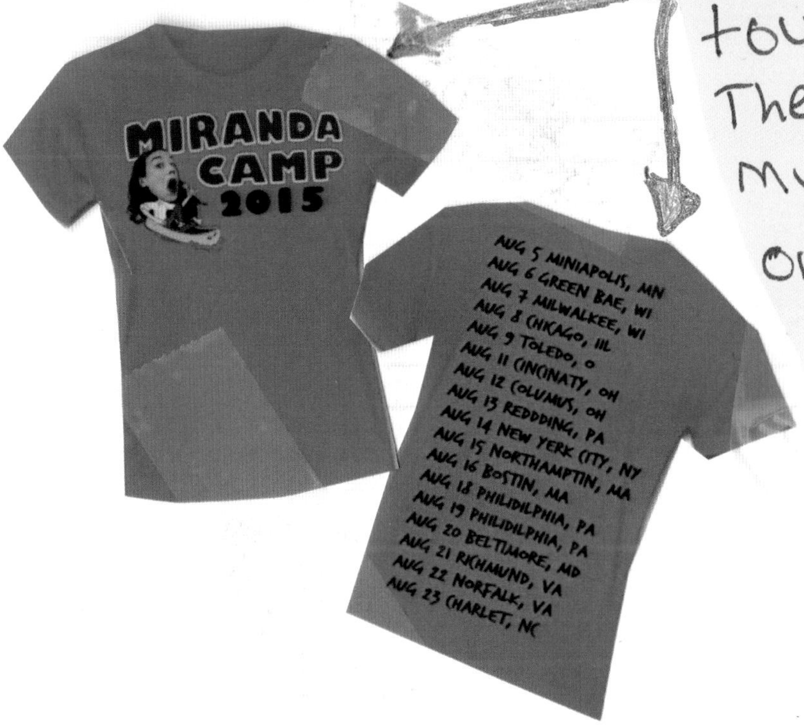

This is what the stage looks like! its like actual summer camp Butt Better! cuz im at it.

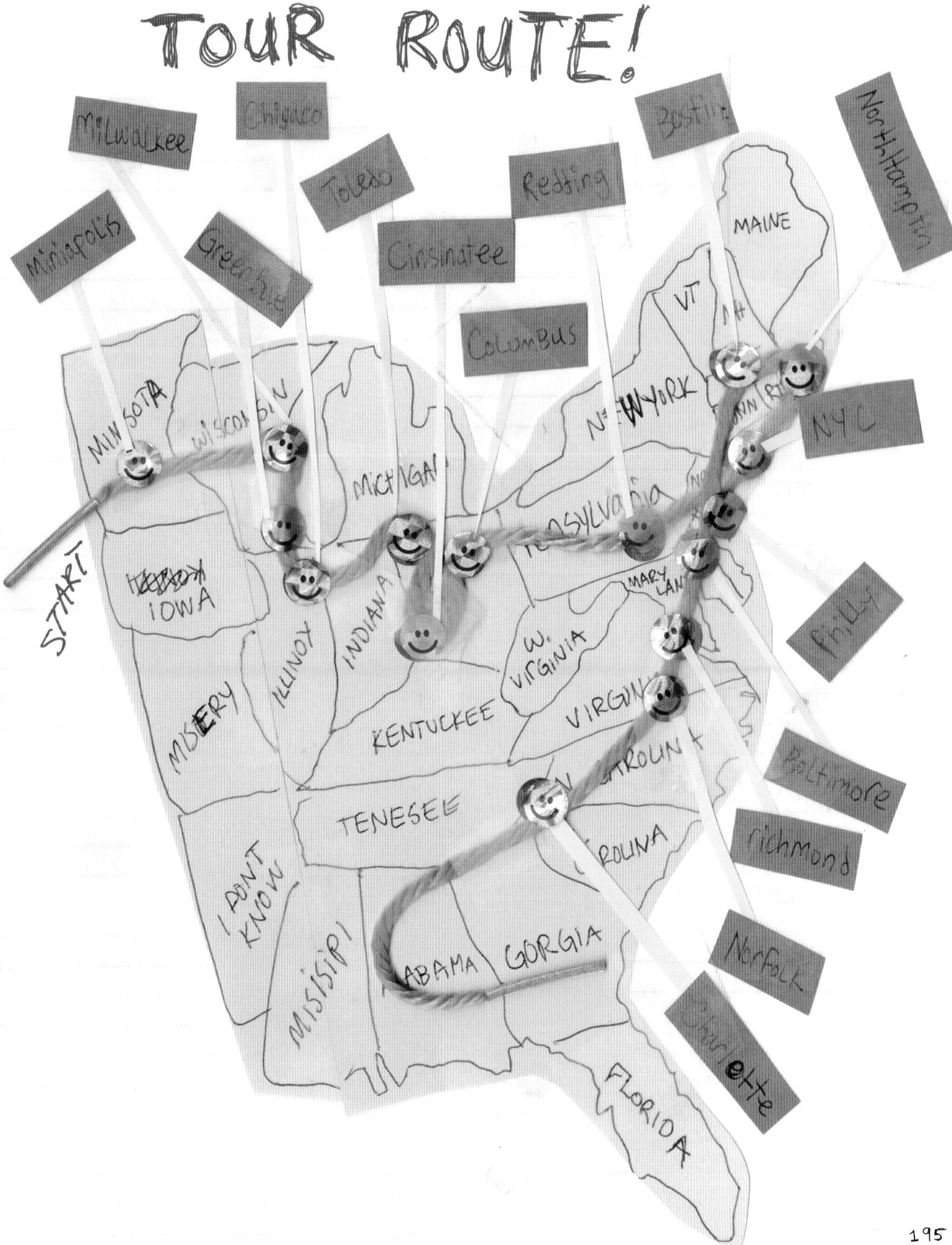
TOUR ROUTE!
START
Miniapolis
Milwalkee
Chigaco
Toledo
Cinsinatee
Columbus
Redding
Bostin
NorthHamptin
NYC
Philly
Boltimore
richmond
Norfolk
Charlotte
MAINE
VT
NEW YORK
MINSOTA
WISCONSIN
MICHIGAN
IOWA
ILLINOY
INDIANA
W. VIRGINIA
VIRGINIA
KENTUCKEE
MISERY
TENESEE
I DONT KNOW
MISISIPI
ABAMA
GORGIA
FLORIDA

Dear Diarrhe,

Miranda Sings
Aug 15, 2015
10:45 PM

Bus tour is Fun, Butt im Freaking Tired! The dum Bus Driver keeps driving while im trying to sleep and its making my Bed move. So RUDE! We are over half way done with tour so i thot it wuld Be good to write down some of the memoraBel moments so Far –

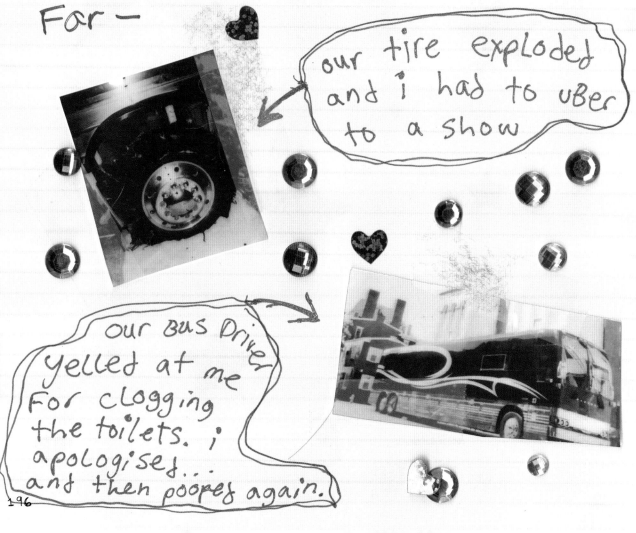

our tire exploded and i had to uBer to a show

our Bus Driver yelled at me For clogging the toilets. i apologised... and then pooped again.

we hired a Lady to give me a massage cuz ive Been VERY stressed and she just Poked my Forehead and heart For a hour and said, "you are healed" over and over. she smelled like mold.

Ben stiller came 2 my NYC show. i dont no who he is Butt every one was Freaking out. i think mayBe this is him

This is what it Looks Like outside my Bus every Nite.

My Buttsistant told me she is quitting soon. So annoying. i dont no why anyone wuld want to quit working with me!

mood: Nothing

Dear Diarrhe,

Miranda Sings
Aug 16, 2015
11:07.5pm

No offense, Butt this has Been one of the craziest nite's of my Life. i FAINTED ON STAGE! Well... tecknickly i wasnt on stage. i Left the stage in the middle of the show cuz i started feeling weird and i passed out rite when i got in the wings. Rachel had to go on stage and intertain the audience while i came Back to Life. i think i almost died probly. The doctor said i just had dehydration Butt i told him that wuld Be impossible cuz im a virgin. Virgins dont get genitel diseases. its a Fact. Then he told me i need to drink more Liquids so this doesn't happen again, Butt i drink Like 7 sodas a day. AND tons of kool-aid. So

Basicly, hes a idiot. i was probly just poisened.

Anyways, After the show, i checked my phone and i had a text from Lilly Singh. it said, "Congrats! You won!" i thot she meant just winning at life so i was like "thanks." Butt then i found out i won A TEEN CHOICE AWARD! While i was fainting i won the most prestigious award a celebrity can win. iCONic. i cant wait to get my surfBord. i always wanted to add "surfing" to my list of talents. gotta go... this Bus is relly Bumpy and i need to poo again.

♡
Miranda

after i fainted i got back on stage and finished the show

mood: tired happy hungry and

Dear Diarrhe,

Miranda Sings
Jan 1, 2016
2:61 pm.

i got home from Bus tour a couple months ago and got **RELLY BUSY** with the NetFLix Show. And since my dumb Buttsistant Rachel **QUIT** i had to hire a New Buttsistant His name is **Kory** and he is relly cute. Hopefully he will get relly Famus so we can date some day. **(as you know, i only date Famus people)** He's good at his joB Butt i relly miss Patrick Being my roadie. i Fired him a Long time ago cuz he cant help me with my quick changes Back stage untill we are married. **PLus he's allergic to milk.**

♡ Miranda

This is Kory. ←

mood: sticky

Dear Diarrhe,

Miranda Sings
APRIL 9, 2016
9:42 PM

OK, so rember how NetFLix told me they wanted to do a show about my Life? WeLL i am TICKED OFF! i thot i wuld just make my own Show and they wuld give me money to do whatever I want. Butt they hired a **cast**, a **crew**, and i have to move to VANCOOVER, Canada. They even gave us scripts! This is so annoying. OH! AND ANOTHER THiNG! They are telling a Bunch of secrets from my Life in this T.V. show! They want to show my SISTER! Ugh. The onLy thing worse wuld Be if my Diarrhe's got Leaked. if that ever happened my LiFe wuld Be **over**! Anyways, i move to Vancoover to start shooting tomorrow. i'LL teLL you how it goes. i hope i understand the Language in Canada.

Miranda

mood: Ticked off and ichy

Dear Diarrhe,

miranda Sings
April 22 2016
3:02 am

we just Finished shooting the First episode. im so Tired! it took 4 days to shoot. That coleen girl is anoying Butt im glad she's hear cuz this is a lot of work and i dont wanna do most ~~seens~~. scenes. (Dont tell her i said that.) Anyways, hear are some pictures from set —

This is the cast. They r all kinda annoying Butt also nice.

They remade the Fish store my uncle worked at. exsept its Fansier and has more Living Fish.

This is the set of my room. i hate it cuz it dosnt have a roof. just Lights.

♡miranda

Mood: exausted

Miranda Sings
May 29, 2016
4:02 a.M.

Dear Diarrhe,

im so **Freaking annoyed!** Filming this show is dum! i will do a scene and the directer will say "cut!" and then make us do it again and again and again! i allready did it once! why do i have to do it a million times? Especially if i Lived it For REAL? So glad its almost over. Butt im essited to have my own Netflix original series.

Miranda is the new BLACK.

Filming episode 2. They got mad cuz i kept singing after they yelled "cut". Butt they shuld have Been THANKING ME! i gave them a free consert!

Me and Patrick. He Looks esactly like him.

♡ miranda

mood: relly ~~happy~~ annoyed

Miranda Sings
Oct 14, 2016
11:54pm

Dear Diarrhe,

Tonite was the **premeer of the NetFLix show.** That dum Collen girl showed up Looking Like a total skank. i could see her entire chestickles. she Looked Like a skin colored sausege Link. → **She's so anoying!** We had a deal and she keeps trying to cum in and steal my thunder, and take all the credit. **She's relly confusing my Fans!** Some of them think shes me! ugh. Anyways, the Show is relly good (OBVIUSLY) and i Love my Fans SO MUCH without them it never wuld have happened. ALSO they give me presents. Gotta go. Mom made a canned Food Buffet to celebrate. ♡ Miranda

mood: happy

Dear Diarrhe,

Miranda Sings
Dec 1, 2016
7:09 PM

im in the land **OF SIN** doing a show yup. **Vegas.** ive Been praying relly hard for all the sinners hear Butt decided to take a Break to Let you no that **NetFLix called** and we are getting a season 2 of Haters Back off! That means i am offishally the first YouTuBer in <u>History</u> to get her own TV show picked up for a second season on NetFLix Called Haters Back off starring Miranda Sings! Butt i relly hope they dont put me in the Guinness Book of world records cuz i do <u>NOT</u> Like Beer.

♡ miranda

P.S. My show in vegas went relly good even tho it was Full of sinners.

Mood: sweaty

Dear Diarrhe,

miranda Sings
April 18, 2017
10:02 pm..

Welp, im on set for **Season 2** of Haters Back OFF, and once again, the crew is making this WAY more harder then it needs to Be. This is why i wanted to do everything myself! ok hears a example—

We are doing a episode about when i wore a taco costume and had a protest.

__So First__— the writers drew the Logo of the taco resterant.

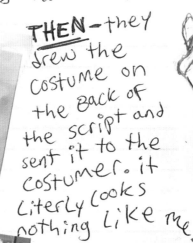

__THEN__—they drew the costume on the Back of the script and the sent it to the costumer. it Literly Looks nothing Like me.

__NEXT__—they made a tiny doll version of the costume

__FINALLY__— i got to ware the costume Like a month Later

__See?__ So over-compicated. i told them to just make it out of paper or just do CGI Butt no one Listened to me. Literaly EVERYTHING in the show is Like this. so **COMPLICATED!** ugh.

mood: every1 is dumB..

♡ Miranda

Dear Diarrhe

miranda Sings
Sep 11, 2017
6:09 pm

i just realized i never even told you about all the collabs i Been doing since i Been getting more Famuser. i Have TONS of new Baes, and some new emenies. Hear are some of the peopol i have collaBed with.

Theres alot more Butt i forgot. Anyways, i got 2 announce the date my NetFLix show season 2 preemeers. it was on a popsickle stick. i Live streemed me eating it... Afterwords i sat alone for 6 hours. sometimes Being me is Lonely. Butt then i realized your never alone if you have food. so i ate more popsickles

♡ miranda

MOOD: Gassy.

octobur 20

Miranda Sings
Oct 21, 2017
4:49 pm

Dear Diarrhe,

Season 2 came out and im incredibol in it, no offense, Butt they DELETED SCENES! There was a scene where i was dancing and singing with all these sexy Boys and it got CUT! Probly cuz i was just too good and it made every1 else Look Bad.

and they also cut a scene where we threw a Birthday party for my mom, and that got cut too!

at Least i have some secret rehersal Footage of ~~Coalen Collen~~ that dum girl doing the dance number... i wish i had Footage of me doing it cuz im WAY Better.

mood: amazing

♡ Miranda

Dear Diarrhe,

Miranda Sings
Dec 15, 2017
~~1:02 pm~~ 1:03 PM

i havent written to you in a while Butt dont worry, not much has happened...

- i interviewed celebrities on the red carpet for **ELLEN**
- i went on the **Jimmy Fallon** show 2 times.
- i was on **"Live with Kelly and Ryan"**
- i hit **8 Million** subscribers on YouTuBe
- i have **6.5 million** insta followers, and **2.7 million** [redacted] twitter followers.
- i didnt get a season 3 of **Haters Back off**.
- i pretended like i didnt care Butt i cried alot.
- i went on a **sold out world tour**.
- i found a **flea** on my cat.
- i got a lot more famus **Boy frends**
- got nominated for a Bunch of awards.
- i got a hangnail on my pinky toe wich i didnt even know was possiBol.

See? Not much happened. Butt this pinky toe hangnail situation is relly upsetting me. i tried ripping it out Butt it started to Bleed. **Ugh..** Jesus Take the Wheel! **why does Bad stuff always happen to good people?!?**

please pray 4 me.

♡ Miranda

mood: Bloody.

Miranda Sings
Jan 1, 2018

Well Diarrhe,

ive Been doing alot of thinking lately and its exhausting. Butt also i realized something. When i First started out on YouTuBe no one respected YouTuBers. No One would take us seriusly. Butt the whole internet comunity knew that if we just worked hard, stayed Patient, and found success, **one day**... we wuld Be respected. **One day**... we wuld Be taken seriusly. **One Day**... we wuld get the recognition we deserve. Well Diarrhe, ive Been on YouTuBe for 10-ish years and **the day is Finally here**... where i realize its never gonna happen. its 2018 and the only YouTuBers in the news are rich young white Boys doing relly Bad immature stuff. They are making the rest of us Look Bad... And it is **HARD** to make me Look Bad. →

Now im no scientist Butt last time i checked, i wasnt a rich, young, immature white Boy so i gotta Figure out a way to stay **Famus!** Now i obviusly conkered **YouTuBe**, NetFLix, world Tours, merch, relationships, and writing a Book, so its time for me to get creative and plan out the next Big thing in my career. So hear are some of my **TOP SECRET** ideas to Becum a Famus iconic Legend.

Viral video ideas

- stare at camera without BLinking for 30 minutes challenge
- Try Fitting whole Foot in mouth challenge.
- eat Lunch

Tours

i allready Been to Europe, Austrailia, New Zeeland, america, and Canada. im pretty sure thats the hole earth. So my Next tour... will Be in **SPACE!**

Movies

★ i dont no how this is possible Butt i still havent made a movie. it has to Be **BIG** so i need to think outside the Box and Be original. Sooo... hear's what im thinking. Everyone makes movies with awake people. So im gonna do a whole movie of me sleeping! it will Be iconic cuz no one has done it Before #genious

invenchons

★ This is the most exciting thing of all. im gonna start inventing stuff so i can add **inventer** to my talent list. Hear are some of my genious invenchons so far...

★THE SLEEP IN ALARM★

what does everyone want? **MORE SLEEP!** so i want to invent a alarm that goes off 2 hours after the time you set for it to go off. That way you get **2** more hours of sleep Butt no one can get mad at you if your late to stuff cuz it was the alarms fault. #Geniousinvenchom

★BATH BOMB DiNNER★

Everyone Loves Bath BOMBS and everyone Loves eating, so i want to comBine the two. Bath BOMBS usually just squirt out a color, Butt how cool would it Be if they squirted out a taco?! or a Burrito? or Lasania? You could take a Bath and go under water with your mouth open and get a mouthFull of ground Beef. im gonna make a ~~FORCHUNE~~ FORTUNE!

★EDiBLE MOLD★

im sick of throwing away perfectly good Food just Becuz mom said it got some mold on it. So i want to invent ediBle mold! Your Food will never go Bad again! it will just get delishiously Fuzzy.

imagine if all this delishious FOOD squirted out of a Soapy Ball!

STAY ASLeep ALARM!
imagine waking up WAY AFTER your alarm. #GOALS

imagine eating this Fuzzy treat!

So Diarrhe, as you can see, i have some pretty amazing plans and my career is about to **EXPLODE!** Oh! And guess what else? i dont have Haters anymore! i realized the people saying mean and rude things about me arent Haters at all! They are actually **SUPER FANS!** Think about it. They wach all my videos, they always comment, they always tweet me, they know everything about me, and they are totally obsessed with me. **THATS A FAN!** So to all those haters who keep saying "give up!" or "get off YouTube" or "go away No one Likes you", **DONT WORRY.** i will never stop working hard and Being Famus cuz i no **YOU** would miss me the most.

Gotta go. mom made tator tots for dinner and i have a scab to pick.

♡

Miranda

[redacted]

P.S. im perfect.

mood:
unstopable
happy
grateful
hopfull
gassy

YouTube personality **Miranda Sings**, created by comedian Colleen Ballinger, is a hilariously underwhelming 'singer, model, actor, dancer and magician'. Known for her comically toneless singing, terrible advice and in-your-face red lipstick (applied well outside her lips, of course), Miranda never fails to elicit hysterical laughter. From collaboration with super 'Mirfanda' Jerry Seinfeld and drawing millions of fans around the world to her live performances to creating, producing, writing and starring in two seasons of her own Netflix Original series, *Haters Back Off*, Miranda dominates both the 'innernet' scene and audiences all over the world.